SOUTHERN LITERARY STUDIES

Fred Hobson, Editor

COMIC VISIONS, FEMALE VOICES

Comic Visions, Female Voices

Contemporary Women Novelists and Southern Humor

BARBARA BENNETT

Louisiana State University Press / Baton Rouge

Designer: Glynnis Weston
Typefaces: text: Bembo; display: Randumhouse
Typesetter: Wilsted & Taylor Publishing Services
Printer and binder: Edwards Brothers, Inc.

Grateful acknowledgment is made to Doris Betts, Josephine Humphreys, and Lee Smith for
permission to reproduce excerpts from their letters to the author.

Library of Congress Cataloging-in-Publication Data

Bennett, Barbara, 1959–
    Comic visions, female voices : contemporary women novelists and
Southern humor / Barbara Bennett.
        p.   cm. — (Southern literary studies)
    Includes bibliographical references (p.   ) and index.
    ISBN 0-8071-2288-2 (cloth : alk. paper)
        1. Humorous stories, American—Southern States—History and
criticism.   2. American wit and humor—Southern States—History and
criticism.   3. American wit and humor—Women authors—History and
criticism.   4. Women and literature—Southern States—History—20th
century.   5. American fiction—Women authors—History and criticism.
6. American fiction—20th century—History and criticism.
7. Southern States—In literature.   8. Comic, The, in literature.
I. Title.   II. Series.
PS261.B46   1998
813′.54099287—dc21   98-20584
                                                       CIP

for my sister
JULIA

CONTENTS

ACKNOWLEDGMENTS

Many people deserve thanks for helping me during the writing of this book. Several professors at Arizona State University—Thelma Shinn Richard, D. G. Kehl, and Don L. F. Nilsen—gave me excellent advice and direction in the very early stages. I am also grateful to Robert W. Jones for listening to my frequent whining and offering an absorbent shoulder throughout the process.

For special friendship, I wish to thank Kathleen Godfrey, Jacquelyn Scott Lynch, Nancy Houston, and Joanne Boland. Not only do these women support me, but they also remind me to laugh. For personal sanity and inspiration, I owe a great deal to Carolyn A. Jones, who helped me discover my own voice and learn how to use it, and Gail Griffin, whose words and ideas sustain me daily.

I also wish to express my gratitude to John Easterly at Louisiana State University Press for his unwavering encouragement. Finally, I owe special thanks to Fred Hobson for sharing his knowledge, his talent, and his time.

ABBREVIATIONS

AI	Almost Innocent	IC	In Country
B	Bingo	K	Kinflicks
BC	Bastard out of Carolina	OH	Oral History
BF	Baby of the Family	OW	Other Women
BL	Breathing Lessons	RD	The Track of Real Desires
BMB	Black Mountain Breakdown	RJ	Rubyfruit Jungle
BR	Bedrock	RL	Rich in Love
BT	The Bean Trees	RLG	The Revolution of Little
C	The Cheer Leader		Girls
CP	The Color Purple	S	Starcarbon
CW	The Clock Winder	SD	Southern Discomfort
DF	Daisy Fay and the Miracle Man	SF	She Flew the Coop
		SL	Southern Ladies and
EF	Ellen Foster		Gentlemen
EL	Charms for the Easy Life	SO	Six of One
EP	Earthly Possessions	SP	Slow Poison
FB	Ferris Beach	TC	The Tin Can Tree
FGT	Fried Green Tomatoes	TE	Their Eyes Were Watching
FS	Fancy Strut		God
FSL	Confessions of a Failed Southern Lady	TOW	The Odd Woman
		TV	Tending to Virginia
HOP	Her Own Place	UW	Ugly Ways
HR	Dinner at the Homesick Restaurant	VE	Venus Envy
		W	Who Do You Love?
HW	Heading West		

COMIC VISIONS, FEMALE VOICES

INTRODUCTION

Southern Laughter and the Woman Writer

Laughter I declare to be blessed; you who aspire to greatness, learn how to laugh!

—FRIEDRICH NIETZSCHE

Being humorous in the South is like being motorized in Los Angeles or argumentative in New York—humorous is not generally a whole calling in itself, it's just something that you're in trouble if you aren't.

—ROY BLOUNT

Dorothy Allison has described herself as "sharp, squint-eyed, determined, too caustic, stubbornly hopeful and occasionally funny as hell."[1] Allison's final phrase is perhaps the most unexpected, coming from a writer who deals with such unpleasant subjects as child abuse. Yet "funny" is an adjective that describes Allison as well as many other contemporary southern women writers, although the humor in these writers' works has long been overlooked and underappreciated, especially in the traditionally male-dominated literary world.

To be fair, literary humor in general—in male or female authors—has not received its deserved critical attention, even though, as Louis D. Rubin, Jr., points out in *The Comic Imagination in American Literature,* "There is scarcely an important American writer who does not at one time or another see the problem before him comically." This neglect is not limited to the study of literature: Freud noted that "jokes have not received nearly as much philosophical consideration as they deserve in view of the part they play in our mental life."[2] One reason humor has received such short shrift from critics is that comedy is commonly believed to be less important, and therefore less deserving of analysis, than tragedy. The ever-present Puritan within many Americans equates significance with sobriety, with the result that so-called serious writers are more highly praised than comic ones.

1. Dorothy Allison to the author, December 7, 1993.
2. Louis D. Rubin, Jr., ed., *The Comic Imagination in American Literature* (New Brunswick, N.J., 1973), viii; Sigmund Freud, *Jokes and Their Relation to the Unconscious,* trans. James Strachey (New York, 1963), 5.

Southern humor has received about the same amount of attention as most other regional humor. Studies of southern humor in the nineteenth century have mainly focused on male authors—humorists of the Old Southwest and, of course, Mark Twain. As Merrill Skaggs points out, however, a "startling high percentage of the Southern writers publishing in the late nineteenth century were female."[3] In studies of twentieth-century southern humor, fair consideration has been given to Eudora Welty, Flannery O'Connor, and Carson McCullers, along with William Faulkner, but little has been published about the humor of contemporary southern writers and even less about women writers. The question could be asked if this subject is worthy of study, and the answer is "yes," for several reasons. Humor is an intricate part of many southern women writers' works, helping to define voice, communicate theme, and establish new definitions of southern literature; the tone is often more optimistic and less guilt ridden than that found in fiction written by men or by their literary predecessors. In addition, most female humor has a distinct voice and vision: iconoclastic, yet ultimately unifying; challenging traditional relationships, yet affirming the self and family.

The three issues that are most significant in this study are the "southernness" of the writing, the contemporary setting, and the female perspective. Each is intrinsic to the new voice and vision that women writers bring to the literature of today's South, and in all three, humor plays an important role. Despite its importance, though, humor is difficult to define, and in making the attempt, critics often experience frustration of the sort expressed by Dorothy Parker, who claimed that every time she tried, she "had to go and lie down with a cold wet cloth on [her] head."[4] Definitions of regional humor are even more difficult to isolate and clarify, usually tending toward generalizations. For example, the seven articles in a 1995 issue of *Southern Cultures* dedicated to southern humor deal with topics ranging from folk humor to African American humor to sexual humor and beyond; but not one writer clearly defines southern humor—or even seriously attempts to—most simply list various characteristics of it. In one article, John Shelton Reed concludes that humor "seems to be one of those 'idiomatic imponderables,'" claiming only that southern humor is "different—different enough that others don't always understand it."[5]

Perhaps the ability to define southern humor is not as important as the

3. Merrill Skaggs, "Varieties of Local Color," in *The History of Southern Literature,* ed. Louis D. Rubin, Jr. (Baton Rouge, 1985), 219.

4. Dorothy Parker, Introduction to *The Most of S. J. Perelman,* by S. J. Perelman (New York, 1958), xii.

5. John Shelton Reed, "The Front Porch," *Southern Cultures,* I (1995), 418.

capacity to recognize it and distinguish it from other types of humor. Reed comes closest to describing southern humor when he quotes Jerry Clower: "I don't tell funny stories. I tell stories funny." An important characteristic, then, of southern humor is what Lee Smith calls "a love of storytelling for its own sake."[6] Twain said much the same thing in his essay "How to Tell a Story," observing that a "humorous story may be spun out to great length, and may wander around as much as it pleases, and arrive nowhere in particular." This narrative pattern can be found in his most famous short story, "The Notorious Jumping Frog of Calaveras County." Here the humor is derived mainly from the inclusion of absurd details, from the contrast between the two narrators—both of whom appear ridiculous—and from the seemingly meaningless meanderings of farfetched subplots. One doesn't look for the point of the story; the story *is* the point.

If this is true, the topic of a southern humorous story can be almost anything, and in *Roy Blount's Book of Southern Humor,* Blount lists some possibilities: "dirt, chickens, defeat, family, religion, prejudice, collard greens, politics, and diddie wa diddie."[7] By putting defeat and religion on a par with dirt and collard greens, Blount supports the claim that the humor is in the telling, not in the topic, and his inclusion of the nebulous "diddie wa diddie" implies an inability to articulate what is humorous—as well as the oral quality to southern humor. Despite Blount's encompassing list, some subjects and situations do surface more often than others in southern humor: death and violence, scatology, religion, sex, gender roles, and the place of tradition in contemporary life. Of course, these topics are not exclusively southern, but southerners—and southern women writers in particular—approach them in a distinct style.

In addition, southern humor often depends on a certain voice, tone, and use of language—which is one reason so many southern stories are told in the first person. Such stories seem meant to be read aloud, and as narrators tell their tales, readers do not just read: they hear. Again, Twain's story serves as an excellent example: when the second narrator, Simon Wheeler, begins his final tale with the words, "Well, thish-yer Smiley had a yaller one-eyed cow that didn't have no tail, only just a short stump like a bannanner," the reader laughs—not at the pathetic, afflicted cow but at the tone, the voice, the vivid language, and the fresh details.

This example highlights another important quality in southern humor: it often rises out of tragedy. If this is true, it is not surprising that writers in the South have been so prolific in creating humorous literature. Some

---

6. *Ibid.,* 418–19; Lee Smith to the author, December 9, 1993.
7. Roy Blount, Jr., ed., *Roy Blount's Book of Southern Humor* (New York, 1994), 24.

scholars cite the Civil War as a strong factor contributing to the development of a unique humor in the South. Paradoxically enough, war does not initiate tragic creations as often as comic ones, according to Sarah Blacher Cohen, who argues that the South's defeat in the Civil War gave rise to one of the two periods of "the greatest burgeoning of American comedy"—the Depression being the other—because "travail gives rise to humor, which expresses people's rage at the senseless turn of events and dissipates their gloom." Rubin further explains this connection between tragedy and comedy: "The South has been caught up in a process of transition which has been marked by considerable turmoil and ugliness. Its literature has been one of the happier products of this process. Not merely along with, but indeed *directly out of* the turmoil and even the violence of the changing South, there have come novels and poems which have fixed the image of the South in art and have given to it the imaginative dignity of tragedy and comedy." Numerous critics and philosophers have commented on the power of humor during times of misfortune, both as respite from pain and as aid in recovery. Henri Bergson, for example, asserts that comedy produces "a momentary anesthesia of the heart." Wylie Sypher claims that "comedy is essentially a Carrying Away of Death."[8] Defeat and despair are not exclusively southern, of course, which may be one reason the literature of the South has been so popular with nonsouthern readers.

One cannot rely too heavily on tragedy and despair resulting from the Civil War as an explanation of southern humor, however, especially when analyzing southern women's humor: As women scholars have pointed out, the response to the Civil War was much different for white women than for white men. Anne Goodwyn Jones argues that southern white women, instead of being broken and depressed by the war, "gained the self-reliance and sense of competence that comes from useful work during and after the Civil War." Doris Betts muses that subsequent generations of these writers did not grow up listening to Civil War stories on front porches because they were instead probably "out in the detached kitchens baking pies at storytime."[9]

---

8. Sarah Blacher Cohen, ed., *Comic Relief: Humor in Contemporary American Literature* (Urbana, Ill., 1978), 1; Louis D. Rubin, Jr., *William Elliott Shoots a Bear: Essays on the Southern Literary Imagination* (Baton Rouge, 1975), 256; Henri Bergson, "Laughter" (1900), rpr. in *Comedy,* ed. Wylie Sypher (Garden City, N.Y., 1956), 64; Sypher, *Comedy,* 220.

9. Anne Goodwyn Jones, *Tomorrow Is Another Day: The Woman Writer in the South, 1859–1936* (Baton Rouge, 1981), 25; Doris Betts, "Daughters, Southerners, and Daisy," in *The Female Tradition in Southern Literature: Essays on Southern Women Writers,* ed. Carol S. Manning (Champaign, Ill., 1993), 266.

Civil War stories were quite different for freed slaves as well, since, unlike white southerners, they did not lose the war, and their contributions to southern humor are often overlooked completely. Johanna Nicol Shields believes that the roots of the humor of the Old Southwest lie in the trickster figure common in slave stories, which were often based on African tales. Trudier Harris sees African American humor as stemming not from the Civil War but from slaves who used laughter as a way to avoid tears, a technique she calls "the blues motif": "Put simply, for African Americans, humor made the South not only endurable but transcendable, for humor reduced the South to a laughably manageable level of insanity."[10] Whichever theory or combination of theories one chooses, the link between comedy and tragedy is undeniable, and although tragedy is not exclusively southern, the southerner's penchant for certain types of humor, such as gallows humor, may be directly related to feelings of defeat that, in the United States, only the South has experienced.

The southerner's tie to the past is powerful, and therefore any study of contemporary southern literature must cast at least a brief glance backward. And although there are many comprehensive studies of southern literary history, it is worthwhile here to look at the writers and movements that have influenced the ways today's women writers employ humor.

The history of southern humor begins with the history of southern literature itself. In the seventeenth and eighteenth centuries, southern writers produced a great deal of satire, but as William Ferris argues, the satire was not regionally unique; it was mainly an imitation of eighteenth-century European neoclassical comedy.[11] A uniquely southern literature did not exist until about 1840, when economic, political, and social conditions in the North and the South began to diverge and the South emerged as a distinct region.

Roughly twenty to thirty years before the Civil War, the oral tradition met print and publication in the humor of the Old Southwest. This fiction, from a region that includes what is now considered the Deep South, was written and read almost exclusively by white men. It is characterized by tall tales rife with exaggeration and the boastful recounting of humorous events, usually in the dialect of the uneducated but imaginative southwestern narrator. In a 1964 study, Hennig Cohen and William Dillingham

---

10. Johanna Nicol Shields, "White Honor, Black Humor, and the Making of a Southern Style," *Southern Cultures,* I (1995), 421; Trudier Harris, "Adventures in a 'Foreign Country': African American Humor and the South," *Southern Cultures,* I (1995), 458.

11. William Ferris, "Southern Literature and Folk Humor," *Southern Cultures,* I (1995), 431.

identify the subjects, themes, and characteristics common to these humorists, many of which emerge in the writings of other nineteenth- and twentieth-century southern writers. In terms of far-reaching influences on contemporary female writers, the most salient of these include an oral quality to the tales, delight in the vivid and concrete, the frequent use of a first-person narrator, the use of black or "unhealthy" humor, and an attempt to "record realistically local customs and manners and to provide a chronicle of the times."[12]

Cohen and Dillingham describe the humor of this period as essentially "masculine" in comparison to the "genteel literature which was being enjoyed by pale young ladies in New England drawing rooms." Apparently this label was assigned because of the sometimes earthy nature of the humor, which showed a "lack of respect for delicate sensibilities";[13] however, female characters created by those male writers are far from resembling those protected and "pale" New Englanders. In the following excerpt from *The Crockett Almanacs,* entitled "Crockett's Daughters," readers discover a woman who is feisty, strong, and independent: "An' I guess I shall never forget how all horrificaciously flumexed a hull party of Indians war, the time they surprised and seized my middle darter, Thebeann. . . . The varmints knew as soon as they got hold of her that she war one of my breed, by her thunderbolt kickin', and they determined to cook half of her and eat the other half alive, out of revenge for the many lickin's I gin 'em."[14] Although such characters might not appeal to New England "ladies," it is easy to identify Thebeann's spirit in such twentieth-century literary sisters as Carson McCullers' Miss Amelia, Flannery O'Connor's Mary Grace, Fannie Flagg's Idgie Threadgoode, and Rita Mae Brown's Molly Bolt, among others, all of whom appeal to modern women readers.

Mark Twain was influenced by the humorists of the Old Southwest in several ways. Following in their patterns but refining and sharpening their techniques, Twain created literature that is far superior. In Twain's work, James Cox has identified the southwestern humorist's habit of putting "enormous imaginative pressure on both the gentleman and the bumpkin." Hugh Holman has noted the "detached, cool, amused, generally tolerant, and often sardonic" tone of the typical narrator; Pascal Covici, Jr., has remarked on another similarity: "A character is pushed by the author into a situation in which he either exposes the pretensions of others or himself

12. Hennig Cohen and William B. Dillingham, *Humor of the Old Southwest* (Boston, 1964), xiii.

13. *Ibid.,* xi, xiv.

14. Richard M. Dorson, ed., *Davy Crockett: American Comic Legend* (New York, 1977), 22.

emerges as ridiculous because of his pretentious behavior."[15] These aspects of Twain's writing—style, tone, and topic—have had a tremendous influence on contemporary women writers, perhaps more than the work of any other writer, male or female.

This is not to say that female authors were not prolific in the nineteenth century. Jones claims that southern women writers have "had an active and highly visible history since colonial times" and that "the South has historically accepted and praised its women writers." There are some problems with this statement, however.[16] First, despite the praise Jones mentions, until fairly recently women writers have not been adequately represented in anthologies of southern writing or mentioned in critical essays, partly because most of the writing that women produced was nonfiction—letters, diaries, journals—and much of it was published in periodicals and hence not preserved.[17] Second, fiction that included humor—by such authors as Mary Noailles Murfree, Sherwood Bonner, Sarah Barnwell Elliott, and Ruth McEnery Stuart—was often relegated to the genre of "local color," a label that connotes inferior fiction with a short lifespan for a limited audience. But the works of these women do not fit neatly into either the category of humor of the Old Southwest or that of local color. Kathryn McKee claims that these writings constitute "a previously unidentified genre" sharing characteristics with both groups. The writers whom McKee labels "Female Local Humorists" were heavily influenced by the humorists of the Old Southwest in their style, their "irreverent and ironic" tone, their regional settings, and their use of humor. But their perspective was decidedly female, allowing them to view their region in a unique way and to "redefine Southern womanhood" in the process.[18]

Despite the ironic tone they shared with the humorists of the Old Southwest, these writers have been categorized as local colorists simply be-

15. James M. Cox, "Humor of the Old Southwest," in *The Comic Imagination in American Literature,* ed. Rubin, 104; C. Hugh Holman, "Detached Laughter in the South," in *Comic Relief,* ed. Cohen, 90; Pascal Covici, Jr., *Mark Twain's Humor: The Image of a World* (Dallas, 1962), 8.

16. Jones, *Tomorrow,* 41.

17. Richard H. King's *A Southern Renaissance: The Cultural Awakening of the South, 1930–1955* includes only Lillian Smith; Richard Croom Beatty identifies only one pretwentieth-century woman writer in *The Literature of the South* (Glenview, Ill., 1968); Jay Broadus Hubbel includes only five women in his bibliography *The South in American Literature, 1607–1900* (Durham, 1954); and *The Literary South* (Baton Rouge, 1979), edited by Louis B. Rubin, Jr., gives a weak overview of women's contributions.

18. Kathryn B. McKee, "Writing in a Different Direction: Women Authors and the Tradition of Southwestern Humor, 1875–1910" (Ph.D. dissertation, University of North Carolina at Chapel Hill, 1996), 25, 24, 23.

cause they are not male. Moreover, it has been male scholars who have generally assigned them this label, falsely assuming that men's writing has universal appeal, whereas women's writing only appeals to women. Carol S. Manning remarks on this practice of excluding women writers from collections, even though nineteenth-century men who wrote "popular, sentimental, inferior fiction" were included in such anthologies. She argues that women writers of the late nineteenth century, like Ellen Glasgow and Kate Chopin, actually began the Southern Renaissance by questioning and asserting themselves through their fiction but were overlooked because they lacked the "central circle of writers or central locale to draw the critics' spotlight" that the Fugitives had in Nashville.[19]

Thanks to the recent work of mostly female scholars, many of these women writers are being rediscovered and are finding their way back into print. Augusta Jane King, Grace King, Alice Dunbar-Nelson, and Frances Newman—as well as dozens of other authors—are finally being recognized and their works analyzed as yet another perspective from which to view the South.[20] One of these rediscovered texts is a wonderfully satiric novel by Ellen Glasgow, *The Romantic Comedians,* first published in 1926, but long out of print and unavailable until the University Press of Virginia reissued it in 1995. The novel is the first and best of what Glasgow called her "trilogy of tragicomedies," focusing on many of the same issues women writers now address: gender differences, relationships, patriarchal images of women, and the changing South.[21] Much of the novel is viewed through the eyes of Judge Honeywell, a man who claims to know everything worth knowing about life and women. Glasgow's tone, much like Twain's, is amused, detached, and ironic, and when Honeywell makes such statements as, "If there is anything wrong with the Episcopal Church or the Democratic Party, I would rather die without knowing it," one is amused at both his naïveté and his arrogance.[22] Interestingly, although other books by Glasgow have remained in print—such as *Barren Ground,* a book virtually devoid of humor—this novel has not, which may be more proof of the lack of respect accorded comedy by literary circles.

Another overlooked satirist is Frances Newman, author of *The Hard-Boiled Virgin* (1930) and *Dead Lovers Are Faithful Lovers* (1928). Although her

19. Manning, ed., *Female Tradition,* 3, 49.

20. For a detailed description of the work being done in the rediscovery of women's literature, I suggest reading Thadious M. Davis' essay, "Women's Art and Authorship in the Southern Region: Connections," *Ibid.,* 15–36.

21. The other two novels in the trilogy are *They Stooped to Folly* (1929) and *The Sheltered Life* (1932).

22. Ellen Glasgow, *The Romantic Comedians* (1926; rpr. Charlottesville, Va., 1995), 8.

books remained out of print until the 1980s, their relevance may simply be that they exist, evidence that women have long questioned the stereotypes of southern womanhood. In *The Hard-Boiled Virgin,* Newman exposes the superficiality of the life of the southern belle who pursues social acceptance at the expense of intellectual growth and individual achievement. Newman's prose is demanding, innovative, and sometimes impossibly convoluted, but the reader is rewarded for persevering with satiric gems such as this: "She did not suspect either the social or the biological soundness of his demonstration that southern gentlemen consider alcoholic beverages unsuited to the fragile organisms which are capable of nothing more energetic than producing twelve babies."[23] Such relatively obscure novels as *The Hard-Boiled Virgin* and *The Romantic Comedians* demonstrate that contemporary satire is merely an extension of the questioning of male and female roles that has been going on for some time; the women's movement of the 1970s only increased its strength and momentum.

A better-known author is William Faulkner, and although his presence is keenly felt in southern literary history, his work has not influenced female writers as much as it has male writers. In my own relatively informal surveys of contemporary women authors, O'Connor and Welty are mentioned more often than any others; for example, when asked about influences on her work, Dorothy Allison simply answered, "Flannery O'Connor, lord yes!" Other writers whose names appear often include Zora Neale Hurston, Harper Lee, Reynolds Price, and Walker Percy, but only Josephine Humphreys mentioned Faulkner—and then only near the end of a list of six authors. Paul Binding, a British writer who did a series of interviews with southern authors in 1979, came to a similar conclusion in his study. He claims that no writers he spoke with praised Faulkner, but virtually all mentioned Welty's work as a "creative example." Is this pattern simply a result of a fear of being compared with one of the greatest twentieth-century American writers? After all, as O'Connor noted, "Nobody wants his mule and wagon stalled on the same track the Dixie Limited is roaring down." Are contemporary writers protesting too much? Perhaps, but probably not. In terms of tone and themes that affirm life, love, and human potential, contemporary women writers are certainly, as Fred Hobson notes, "more nearly apostles of Welty than of Faulkner."[24]

In fact, exorcising Faulkner's influence from their work seems to be a

---

23. Frances Newman, *The Hard-Boiled Virgin* (New York, 1930), 110–11.

24. Paul Binding, *Separate Country: A Literary Journey Through the American South* (New York, 1979), 148; Flannery O'Connor, *Mystery and Manners,* ed. Sally Fitzgerald and Robert Fitzgerald (New York, 1961), 45; Fred Hobson, *The Southern Writer in the Postmodern World* (Athens, Ga., 1991), 78.

preoccupation of many southern writers, who understandably feel burdened at times by his still larger-than-life presence. But women writers do not feel as threatened by the reputations of Welty and O'Connor, who are much less acknowledged and praised by critics, and writers often give a nod in their direction as a sign of appreciation. Valerie Sayers, for example, names two streets in her recurrent setting of Due East, South Carolina, O'Connor Street and Welty Street (on which can be found a restaurant called The Golden Apple), but her references to Faulkner are not so kind: few characters have read his work, and if they have, they do not understand him. In *The Track of Real Desires,* Beverly Lowry does not even mention Faulkner's name, referring ironically to his reputation and near-legendary status by disparaging people who worship him and focusing on Faulkner's role as a tourist attraction whose popularity is rivaled by good southern food: "Scholars and fans who came to the state to visit the shrine of Mississippi's dead genius writer often drove down to Eunola to eat at Moe's, and sometimes people ordered whole cheesecakes."[25] By joking about Faulkner's grip on the South, women writers clear space for themselves and their writing, showing critics that Due East, South Carolina, Hopewell, Kentucky, and Speed, Alabama, are not merely rehashed versions of Yoknapatawpha County.

Numerous writers, northern and southern, male and female, have acknowledged an inspirational indebtedness to Eudora Welty. One of those writers, Lee Smith, has said: "My teachers kept telling me, 'Write what you know' but I didn't know, for a long time, what that was. Then, in Louis Rubin's southern literature class, I came upon the stories of Eudora Welty and Flannery O'Connor. It was as though a literal light bulb snapped on in my head, exactly the way it happens in cartoons."[26] Usually, Welty's keen eye for concrete details, her near-perfect ability to characterize with a single phrase, and her expression of the profound through the simple and mundane are cited by other writers as most influential. Anne Tyler has also acknowledged many times her creative debt to Welty:

> I spent my adolescence planning to be an artist, not a writer. After all, books had to be about major events, and none had ever happened to me. All I knew were tobacco workers, stringing the leaves I handed them and talking up a storm. Then I found a book of Eudora Welty's

---

25. Beverly Lowry, *The Track of Real Desires* (New York, 1994), 19.

26. Lee Smith, "The Voice Behind the Story," in *Friendship and Sympathy: Communities of Southern Women Writers,* ed. Rosemary M. Maggee (Jackson, Miss., 1992), 203.

short stories in the high school library. She was writing about Edna Earle [a character in "The Wide Net"], who was so slow-witted she could sit all day just pondering how the tail of the *C* got through the loop of the *L* on the Coca-Cola sign. Why, I knew Edna Earle. You mean you could *write* about such people?[27]

Welty describes her use of humor as "a way of entry . . . a way to get around something to make it endurable, to live with it or to shrug it off." One reviewer has noted that Welty "possesses the surest comic sense of any American writer alive." Another has said that even though her stories are very funny, the humor is there for the purpose of "providing balance, lending perspective" to the tragedy also apparent in her stories—characteristics clearly evident in the works of today's southern women novelists.[28]

Along with Welty, Flannery O'Connor's influence is acutely felt. Walter Sullivan praises O'Connor as "the only distinctly new and original [voice] to arise in the post-renascence South." Although Sullivan's opinion is undoubtedly overstated, O'Connor's influence on other writers is well documented. Her style, vision, and sense of humor are uniquely her own, however. Hugh Holman describes her conception of a human being as "a frail, weak creature, imperfect and incomplete in all his parts"; such a vision "calls for either comedy or pathos, and pathos was alien to Flannery O'Connor's nature and beliefs."[29] This statement mistakenly puts comedy and pathos at opposite extremes, when in truth, much of O'Connor's satire is aimed at characters whose lack of true religious conviction makes them targets for both pity and comedy, a focus and a technique that contemporary novelists have imitated.

O'Connor's perception that modern life is absurd is certainly apparent in contemporary southern writers, as is her belief that humor can be more than just entertainment and more than just a method for pointing out the deficiencies and inanities of life: it can become the vehicle for transcending the absurd. Many southern women writers have learned this from O'Connor, Welty, Glasgow, and Twain, among others, and although they may

---

27. Anne Tyler, "Still Just Writing," in *The Writer on Her Work,* ed. Janet Sternberg (New York, 1980), 13–14.

28. John Griffin Jones, "Eudora Welty," in *Conversations with Eudora Welty,* ed. Peggy Whitman Prenshaw (Jackson, Miss., 1984), 330; James Boatwright, Review of Eudora Welty's *Losing Battles,* in *New York Times Book Review,* April 12, 1970, p. 1; Ruth M. Vande Kieft, "The Love Ethos of Porter, Welty, and McCullers," in *Female Tradition,* ed. Manning, 245.

29. Walter Sullivan, *Death by Melancholy: Essays on Modern Southern Fiction* (Baton Rouge, 1972), 95; Holman, "Detached," in *Comic Relief,* ed. Cohen, 103.

portray the South and the new role of women within that South differently, echoes of these earlier writers can be found throughout their work. Some aspects of their southern roots have been incorporated into southern novels by women, while other aspects have been acknowledged but subsequently rejected.

The list of literary predecessors who are female humorists is short, for the history of women and humor has been a tale of struggle for recognition and acceptance. Nancy A. Walker, author of "A Very Serious Thing": Women's Humor and American Culture says that "being a female humorist in America has been problematic in a number of ways that are tied closely to other issues in women's history: the tension between intellect and femininity, male and female 'separate spheres,' women's status as a minority group, and the transforming power of a feminist vision." But Walker explains that despite being told that they cannot be funny, women have continued to be "very funny indeed."[30]

Humor tests boundaries and pushes limits, doubly so for women. Although women have always known they could be funny, their humor has mainly been relegated to the kitchen, out of the range of male listeners and on the margins of patriarchal society. Giving voice to that humor in the realm of women is relatively safe, but recording that comic voice on paper is more dangerous and disruptive. Many feminist scholars have acknowledged the subversive nature of writing. In Gail Griffin's 1995 book, Season of the Witch: Border Lines, Marginal Notes, she claims that women instinctively have always known it, even as young girls in school: "I always saw writing, as opposed to speech, as secret, subversive, and immensely powerful, whether I was writing to a friend in class or writing poetry in my notebook instead of watching the film or taking notes. Girls write notes. It is one of the ways their little subversive voices stay alive."[31]

Since "laughter, by definition, explodes conventions," as Merrill Skaggs observes, often taking as its target—at least for women—the powerful and culturally superior, writing combined with laughter would seem to be a revolutionary act. And, in fact, for women it is. Laughter coming from the margins, from the edges, is much more powerful and threatening than laughter coming from the center, as Adrienne Rich has articulated: "Revolutionary art dwells, by its nature, on edges. That is its power: the tension between subject and means, between the is and the what can be." For Anne Jones, "The history of southern women's humor is the history of ex-

---

30. Nancy A. Walker, "A Very Serious Thing": Women's Humor and American Culture (Minneapolis, 1988), 7–8, ix.

31. Gail B. Griffin, Season of the Witch: Border Lines, Marginal Notes (Pasadena, 1995), 196.

panding the limits of what is laughable,"[32] but a more accurate phrasing may be that southern women's humor expands the limits of what is laughable *in the presence of males.* Southern women have always been funny, but until a revolution goes public, it is only the grumblings of the discontented.

Women still face many obstacles in combining writing with humor. Regina Barreca remarks in her introduction to *Last Laughs: Perspectives on Women and Comedy* that critics "do not deny that women have tried to write comedy. They argue instead that women have not been able to do it nearly so well as men." Barreca describes women's comedy as "the attempt to break free of the imposition of 'femininity,'" but the question arises of whose definition of "femininity" and whose standards of writing comedy are being used.[33] If men do not find something funny, does that mean it is *not* funny? If a man does not think a funny woman is feminine, does this mean she is *not* feminine? Researchers have found that men and women find humor in different things and do not always understand each other's jokes, in the same way that people often miss the humor in jokes from other cultures; a cultural gap exists, a lack of common experience. By reevaluating definitions and standards of humor, the study of gender-based comedy becomes an important tool in exploring the differences between the sexes: how we communicate, how we view the world and society, and how we perceive ourselves.

One difference between male and female humor concerns what Emily Toth has termed the "humane humor rule." Her claim is that women target the powerful rather than the powerless and rarely ridicule an aspect of a person or society that cannot be changed. For example, women do not usually attack the physically handicapped, choosing instead to attack those who hold narrowminded attitudes and adhere to cultural stereotypes. An example illustrating how male writers do not follow this "rule" is found in Harry Crews's 1995 novel, *The Mulching of America;* much of Crews's humor is at the expense of unfortunate characters, including the pseudo-divine hare-lipped boss of the Soaps For Life company, who utters such lines as, "My narenip was given na me by Nod!"[34] The character is an authority figure, but instead of attacking his ineffectual leadership, Crews mocks his physical deformity per se, a rare occurrence in female writing.

32. Skaggs, "Varieties," in *History of Southern Literature,* ed. Rubin, 227; Adrienne Rich, *What Is Found There: Notebooks on Poetry and Politics* (New York, 1993), 242; Anne Goodwyn Jones, "The Incredible Shrinking You-Know-What: Southern Women's Humor," *Southern Cultures,* I (1995), 468.

33. Regina Barreca, ed., *Last Laughs: Perspectives on Women and Comedy* (New York, 1988), 5, 6.

34. Harry Crews, *The Mulching of America* (New York, 1995), 11.

Southern women, especially, have had a difficult time being accepted as comic writers, since humor is often linked to intellectual aggression, which directly contradicts the stereotype of southern white females as silent, fragile, and intellectually naïve. Southern black women have had other stereotypes and barriers to overcome as humorists. Racism, cultural differences in determining what is funny, and an inadequate educational background are just a few of the factors that have limited their acceptance. Identifying these stereotypes as false and replacing them with more realistic images of southern women is an ongoing process in which humor plays a major role, a process that is redefining the southern woman.

In the course of untangling contradictions about southern women, Peggy Whitman Prenshaw has identified a "dopplegänger motif" that has created "a parade of Scarletts and Melanies." This pattern, which is not limited to but is certainly widespread in southern literature, is especially interesting in connection with humor. In *They Used to Call Me Snow White . . . But I Drifted: Women's Strategic Use of Humor,* Regina Barreca points out the same polarity found throughout popular culture as well as in literature. Instead of Melanie and Scarlett, Barreca terms the two opposites the "Good Girl" (who doesn't understand sexual jokes, doesn't laugh with her mouth open, and leaves the joke telling to the boys) and the "Bad Girl" (who laughs long and loud, rivals the boys with her own keen sense of humor, and gets all the good lines).[35]

Although Melanies and Scarletts persist in the fiction of the contemporary South, there is a tendency for female authors to bring together these two images in one woman who is both sweet and wicked. Instead of Scarlett and Melanie as rivals, we have Alice Walker's Shug Avery, Rita Mae Brown's Frazier Armstrong, and Kaye Gibbons' Charlie Kate, to name a few, relatively good women by society's standards yet possessing a sharp sense of humor and rebelling to various degrees against the still-patriarchal societies in which they live. What has been true all along for male characters (Rhett Butler, for example, is good, sexy, wicked, and desirable) is finally becoming acceptable for female characters. A sense of humor is becoming not a rarity but a standard characteristic of female protagonists.

A woman with a sense of humor is just one of the similarities of the novels under study here. In addition, all of the writers included consistently use humor to further important themes (themes especially relevant to women), all are southern either by birth or by upbringing, and all use

---

35. Peggy Whitman Prenshaw, "Southern Ladies and the Southern Literary Renaissance," in *Female Tradition,* ed. Manning, 81; Regina Barreca, *They Used to Call Me Snow White . . . But I Drifted: Women's Strategic Use of Humor* (New York, 1991), 3–7.

themes, settings, and characters that are distinctly southern in nature. Finally, these writers have produced the major portion of their work since 1970. This fact is significant. Although most critics make a distinction between modern and postmodern literature, there is ample evidence showing another important break around 1970, especially in southern writing. Changes in literature at that time came about because of two powerful movements: women's liberation and civil rights. Both changed forever the face and the voice of the mainstream southern writer, which now is more often female and African American.

In *The Southern Writer in the Postmodern World,* Hobson explains that it was "in the late 1960s that perceptions and assumptions began to change radically" in the South, producing a decade that "might be seen as pivotal in southern life and letters in much the same way the 1920s was. . . . [A] watershed in southern thought resulted—and, in some ways, a new southern fiction emerged."[36] A talented and exciting group emerged from this era, some of whom are now established authors—for example, Anne Tyler, Lee Smith, and Alice Walker—and others who are just beginning to make a contribution—Dorothy Allison, Tina McElroy Ansa, Sheila Bosworth, Dori Sanders, and Michael Lee West, among others.

There have been several studies on contemporary southern women writers and an increasing number of works on gender and humor, but to my knowledge this is the first study specifically on the use of humor by contemporary southern women novelists.[37] Since humor plays such an important role in these writers' works, it is my hope that this study will be instrumental in identifying and illuminating the voice and vision of the literature of this newest of New Souths.

36. Hobson, *Southern Writer,* 7, 73.

37. Recent studies on contemporary southern women writers that are especially illuminating include Elizabeth J. Harrison's *Female Pastoral: Women Writers Revisioning the American South* (Knoxville, Tenn., 1991), and Linda Tate's *A Southern Weave of Women: Fiction of the Contemporary South* (Athens, Ga., 1994). There are also two significant collections of essays: *Women Writers of the Contemporary South* (Jackson, Miss., 1984) edited by Peggy Whitman Prenshaw, and *Southern Women Writers: The New Generation,* edited by Tonette Bond Inge (Tuscaloosa, 1990). Finally, *Friendship and Sympathy* is an interesting compilation of authors discussing the work of other writers. Among the recent works on gender and humor is Nancy A. Walker's *"A Very Serious Thing,"* which examines the history of American female humor—literary as well as cultural. Regina Barreca continues to write and edit books on women and humor, including *They Used to Call Me Snow White,* which explores the differences between male and female humor.

chapter one

"De Maiden Language":
Voice and Identity

"Lawd!" Phoeby breathed out heavily, "Ah done growed ten
feet higher from jus' listenin' tuh you, Janie."

—ZORA NEALE HURSTON,

Their Eyes Were Watching God

In the South we are not used to woman's speaking.

—MARY JOHNSTON,

IN THE *Atlantic Monthly,*

1910

How women see themselves has changed dramatically during the post-modern era. With expectations from family and society changing, most women have had to redefine who they are and what roles they play in a still male-dominated society. Subsequently, these subjects have been explored in fiction. Many female protagonists attempt to find out how they fit in a patriarchal society while still maintaining their femaleness, with the most important part of this self-discovery being the awareness of their voices—distinct, unique, and female.

Woman as silent presence in the South can be traced to the image of the ideal southern lady so much a part of the South's cultural history, with silence, according to Peggy Whitman Prenshaw, being "the most oppressive and damaging result of the codification of subservience as the essential requisite of the lady." For a woman, finding and using her voice, Thadious Davis claims, is a way "to achieve personhood and independence from subjugation. Telling is a way to achieve authority and autonomy, and it is a way to make peace with the past." Although the patriarchal society of the Old South demanded a woman's public silence, this did not mean that women were quiet, nor did it mean that they did not use humor in a subversive way; they simply confined their voices and humor within the woman's sphere, as Jacquelyn Dowd Hall explains in the preface to *Speaking for Ourselves: Women of the South:* "They formed a secret sisterhood of storytellers and comic artists whose humor functioned as sex education, social criticism, and shared delight."[1]

In the search for and expression of a voice and identity, the use of humor allows a woman to view herself objectively, see her absurdity as well as her beauty, and thus reevaluate her self-image. This power of humor to clarify vision was noted more than a hundred years ago by George Meredith, who claimed that comedy could help people accept that everyone is a bit ridiculous—but still worthy of loving and being loved.[2] Meredith highlights two perspectives: internal and external. First, humor helps a woman see herself more clearly, perhaps redefining who she is against who she wants to be. Second, humor can be a way for a woman to see herself as society sees her, in the process often discovering something new about herself and strengthening her individual voice through the power of language.

For a southern writer, voice and identity are clearly tied to region. As Flannery O'Connor explained in *Mystery and Manners,* the "Southern writer's greatest tie with the South is through his ear, which is usually sharp but not too versatile outside his own idiom. . . . When one Southern character speaks, regardless of his station in life, an echo of all Southern life is heard."[3] Women writers have taken their inspiration from earlier southern novelists like Twain, Faulkner, and Welty, and have cast as their protagonists and narrators ordinary southerners whose voices become as much a part of the story as the story itself.

In both Alice Walker's *The Color Purple* and Lee Smith's *Fair and Tender Ladies,* as Lucinda H. MacKethan notes, the protagonists, Celie and Ivy, write letters to other women. In both novels, the narratives are about the events they report but, more important, they are also about the process of growth and self-discovery that takes place in the letter writers. Their written words become their voices, allowing them to tell stories that would not otherwise be told or appreciated because they are about "female" topics, such as childbearing and homemaking. As MacKethan explains, "The concept of sisterhood—women as protectors, as listeners, as sharers, as cocreators in language—becomes a tangible force through the letters."[4]

In pre-twentieth-century southern literature, woman's voice has been

1. Prenshaw, "Southern," in *Female Tradition,* ed. Manning, 78; Thadious M. Davis, "Alice Walker's Celebration of Self in Southern Generations," in *Women Writers of the Contemporary South,* ed. Peggy Whitman Prenshaw (Jackson, Miss., 1984), 29; Maxine Alexander, ed., *Speaking for Ourselves: Women of the South* (New York, 1984), xi–xii.

2. George Meredith, "An Essay on Comedy" (1877), rpr. in *Comedy,* ed. Sypher, 42.

3. O'Connor, *Mystery,* 199.

4. Lucinda H. MacKethan, *Daughters of Time: Creating Woman's Voice in Southern Story* (Athens, Ga., 1990), 105.

limited. Even into the twentieth century, the female voice is often absent. In Faulkner's *The Sound and the Fury,* for example, each of the first three sections is narrated by one of the Compson brothers. Although Caddy plays an important role in her brothers' lives, her own story—told in her own voice—is conspicuously absent. Faulkner explained that he believed he would lessen Caddy's beauty by allowing her a voice—a disturbing idea, because it equates beauty with silence. And even though the final section in the novel centers on the life of Dilsey, the Compsons' female servant, Dilsey's story is told in third person, in contrast to the brothers' first-person narration. Of both Dilsey's and Caddy's stories, one might ask how these stories can be their own—and be accurate—if they are told by someone else, and especially by a male.

MacKethan explores the development of the female voice from the nineteenth century to the present, focusing on several representative authors; but she does not analyze the emergence of humor in that voice—a significant omission. The silencing of the female voice is also the silencing of the female sense of humor, and finding the southern woman's voice is as much a discovery of her ability to laugh and make others laugh as any other aspect of her life. In the twentieth century, the emergence of female voice begins with the writers who tell a woman's story from her point of view. When a woman writer creates a female storyteller, such as Eudora Welty's Edna Earle in *The Ponder Heart,* that author empowers her character. As the storyteller, such a character determines how and when the story will end, but more important, she also determines how the story will be told. What is included and what is excluded, and how characters and events are presented, are determined by her voice. In creating and telling the story, she creates a self, *her*self, and by making humor part of that self, she becomes a woman with the power not only to endure but also to pass her creative ability on to the next generation of women. Humor can be that powerful.

The power of voice in the process of self-discovery has never been better illustrated than in Zora Neale Hurston's life and work. John Lowe, in *Jump at the Sun: Zora Neale Hurston's Cosmic Comedy,* explores Hurston's own sense of humor as well as its expression in her writing. Sometimes labeled eccentric and criticized for her outspokenness, Hurston, Lowe claims, "suffered some outrageous slings and arrows for being born black and female," but most significantly, "she was silenced for her outrageous sense of humor, something blacks and women were permitted only when it took the most passive forms."[5]

5. John Lowe, *Jump at the Sun: Zora Neale Hurston's Cosmic Comedy* (Urbana, Ill., 1994), 50–51.

Lowe argues that Hurston's humor was "a way to bridge the distances between rural and urban, black and white, rich and poor, man and woman, author and reader," a technique especially evident in *Their Eyes Were Watching God*.[6] The evolution of Janie Crawford's identity is directly related to her understanding of her own voice linked to her sense of humor: knowing its strength, seeing its influence, and learning when to use it. Not until Janie rejects two men who have suppressed her voice and oppressed her identity and met Tea Cake, a man who encourages her to explore the world in which she lives, is Janie able to participate fully in the communal voice by freely expressing her individual voice, and finally bloom like the pear tree that, throughout the novel, has symbolized her secret passions and desires.

Janie claims that Tea Cake "done taught me de maiden language all over," but most important, Tea Cake is also the only man who laughs *with* Janie rather than *at* her; as Hurston puts it, "Their laughter rang out first from the kitchen and all over the house." Tea Cake's first encounter with Janie occurs when he invites her to play checkers with him—something her previous husband had forbidden her to do. As Lowe observes, Tea Cake "wants her to play in every sense of the word."[7] Later, Janie even calls their relationship a "love game" (*TE,* 171). Throughout the novel, there is much comic interplay among the various characters that is generally aggressive, with one character or another serving as "victim" of the joke. But the humor expressed between Janie and Tea Cake is unifying and communal, relying on their mutual love and often communicating feelings that transcend language. Significantly, Tea Cake helps to release Janie's voice and her laughter.

The southern woman's voice has exploded onto the page in the past twenty-five years. Because the South has long been a stronghold of patriarchy, it has taken longer for southern women to get their stories told, but the strength of their voices now is undeniable. Women authors, black and white, dominate the literary South, and their voices are far from the stereotypical soft drawl portrayed in romantic novels. As Doris Betts observes, black and white women have found they have "no taste for watermelon and no balance atop pedestals."[8] Many novels by southern women read like ongoing conversations between the protagonist and the reader. Using an intimate and confessional tone, these writers bring the reader into their stories

6. *Ibid.,* 51.

7. Zora Neale Hurston, *Their Eyes Were Watching God* (1937; rpr. New York, 1990), 109, 102–103; Lowe, *Jump at the Sun,* 178.

8. Doris Betts, Introduction, to *Southern Women Writers: The New Generation,* ed. Tonette Bond Inge (Tuscaloosa, Ala., 1990), 3.

like a confidential friend. This technique is not new in the South or exclusively female. In the first paragraph of *The Adventures of Huckleberry Finn,* Twain establishes the same kind of intimacy between Huck and the reader: "You don't know about me without you have read a book by the name of *The Adventures of Tom Sawyer,* but that ain't no matter." The same tone appears in the twentieth century in the works of Eudora Welty, as in the opening to her comically masterful short story "Why I Live at the P.O.": "I was getting along fine with Mama, Papa-Daddy and Uncle Rondo until my sister Stella-Rondo just separated from her husband and came back home again. Mr. Whitaker! Of course I went with Mr. Whitaker first, when he first appeared here in China Grove, taking 'Pose Yourself' photos, and Stella-Rondo broke us up. Told him I was one-sided. Bigger on one side than the other, which is a deliberate, calculated falsehood: I'm the same." In just the first few lines, the reader is made privy to some of the most personal aspects of the narrator's life, thereby establishing loyalty and intimacy.

Likewise, in the following three openings to contemporary novels, the protagonists confess to secrets of various kinds:

> There is a picture of my mother that she keeps tucked away in her old scrapbook, yellowed pages pressing crumbled corsages, letters, gum wrappers. I used to sneak the book down often just to find that picture, to study every detail.

> When I was little I would think of ways to kill my daddy. I would figure out this or that way and run it down through my head until it got easy.

> I have been afraid of putting air in a tire ever since I saw a tractor tire blow up and throw Newt Hardbine's father over the top of the Standard Oil sign. I'm not lying. He got stuck up there.[9]

Although the protagonists in these novels are very different—one is a soon-to-be orphan from an abusive home; one is a pampered middle-class girl on her way to a nervous breakdown; and one is a Kentucky girl who escapes her southern heritage by moving west to Arizona—the tone in the novels is remarkably similar. After reading the complete novels and listening to the

---

9. Jill McCorkle, *The Cheer Leader* (1984; rpr. Chapel Hill, 1992), 1; Kaye Gibbons, *Ellen Foster* (1987; New York, 1990), 1; Barbara Kingsolver, *The Bean Trees* (1988; rpr. New York, 1989), 1.

voices of these females, one discovers that southern women have much in common: they are full of fears, ambitions, and secrets, many of which are in opposition to the stereotype of a southern lady. In the end, the voices become stronger, often by maintaining a sense of humor through all the changes, rebellions, and tragedies, creating a southern woman whose voice could never be mistaken as weak.

Not only is that voice strong, it is widely heard. Southerners love to talk; it is an established and celebrated fact. In a speech at Georgia College in 1994, Lee Smith described a condition "suffered" by many southern women, which she calls the "Southern Woman's Dreaded Door Disease." The main symptom of this condition is the inability to leave a room full of other southern women without standing at the door, holding the knob, and talking for another fifteen minutes. Intimate and chatty, southern characters say a great deal while seeming to say very little; it is in the subtext, not in the text, that the most important ideas may be found. In *The Track of Real Desires,* Beverly Lowry describes southern conversation in this way: "The trick was to ignore subtext and focus on chatter as if chatter were the point, meantime keeping steady in mind the fact that subtext was everything" (54).

One master of this technique is Anne Tyler, about whose work Joseph C. Voelker has said, "More is heard in its silences, gaps, misunderstandings, and failures to listen than in the words themselves." When Aunt Hattie, one of Tyler's characters in *The Tin Can Tree,* remarks casually about a pushy niece—"She's putting on weight, don't you think?"—the literal and humorous meaning of the text, that is, the weight of the niece, means very little.[10] The subtext, which belittles and minimizes the presence and influence of that niece, is much more important as an illustration of the character of Aunt Hattie and her power and position in the family.

A similar exchange takes place in *Dinner at the Homesick Restaurant* between Cody and his father, who deserted the family but returns years later for his wife's funeral. When the father tells Cody, "I often thought about you after I went away," Cody responds, "Oh? . . . Have you been away?"[11] With this ironic reply, Cody minimizes both the importance of his father's desertion and the significance of his father in his life, subtly punishing him for leaving. Although the dialogue can be seen as humorous, it is also pointed. Without threatening his father or risking a confrontation, Cody uses humor to make his feelings clear.

10.   Joseph C. Voelker, *Art and the Accidental in Anne Tyler* (Columbia, Mo., 1989), 37; Anne Tyler, *The Tin Can Tree* (1965; rpr. New York, 1983), 68.
11.   Anne Tyler, *Dinner at the Homesick Restaurant* (New York, 1982), 298.

Tyler's use of humorous dialogue plays an important role in the extension of a major theme in southern novels by women: the need to communicate. Throughout her thirteen novels, Tyler's characters strain, with varying degrees of success, to connect with others around them. Instead of conversations, Tyler's characters more often have what could be termed "nonversations"—during which the characters let fly at one another and fail to connect or to establish relationships. In *The Accidental Tourist*, Macon's editor, Julian, is doggedly pursuing a personal relationship with Macon and his family. On one occasion, Julian visits Macon and Muriel when Muriel is trying to write country western lyrics for a contest. Julian seems desperate to help her find a line to replace "When we shared every pain," and as Macon is forcing him out the door, Julian tenaciously contributes "When our lives were more sane," "When we used to raise Cain," "When I hadn't met Jane," "When she didn't know Wayne," "When she wasn't inane," "When we guzzled champagne," and "When we stuffed on chow mein."[12] In addition to creating a wonderfully comic scene, Tyler's subtext dramatizes Julian's (and everyone else's) frantic and futile efforts to establish a connection. He knows instinctively that simply by having his words accepted, he will be accepted as a person.

In this scene, the humor is in the text while the subtext reveals theme, but this is not always the case in Tyler's work. She sometimes reverses the two, as in a scene from *Dinner at the Homesick Restaurant* in which Ezra Tull confronts his mother, Pearl, with his fear that he cannot "get in touch with people": "I'm worried if I come too close, they'll say I'm overstepping. They'll say I'm pushy, or . . . emotional, you know. But if I back off, they might think I don't care. I really, honestly, believe I missed some rule that everyone else takes for granted; I must have been absent from school that day. There's this narrow little dividing line I somehow never located." Pearl's ironic response is, "Nonsense; I don't know what you're talking about" (*HR*, 127). Here, the text is about the inability to communicate, and although there is some humor in Ezra's belief that such skills might have been taught at school when he was absent, more significant humor lies in the subtext of his mother's reply. His precise point is that she does not understand him, that he cannot connect with others, a fact that she denies and validates in the same statement. At once pathetic and funny, Ezra is absolutely right about himself.

Another way Tyler extends the theme of miscommunication is through the use of malapropisms—humorous misapplications of words in the place of similarly pronounced ones. Conversations among her characters are rife

---

12. Anne Tyler, *The Accidental Tourist* (1985; rpr. New York, 1986), 248–50.

with linguistic errors; for example, when Janie Rose, a small girl, runs through her nightly prayers saying "Deliver us from measles," the malapropism not only establishes Janie's naïveté but also makes readers laugh (*TC*, 31). Tyler's malapropisms are more than just a humorous device, however; they also show how people desperately want to connect with each other but fail simply out of ignorance. In *Dinner at the Homesick Restaurant,* Ezra is told that a patient in the hospital has a "heart rumor" (*HR*, 188), and in *Breathing Lessons,* Maggie Moran calls her daughter-in-law, Fiona, a "twick."[13] Each of these examples illustrates the different ways that people fail to communicate. Perhaps the sterile atmosphere of the hospital has dehumanized the act of dying until identities and feelings are only inexpressible rumors, and the dying are treated impersonally by those who wait on them. In *Breathing Lessons,* Maggie means to compliment Fiona on her thinness by calling her a "twig" or "stick." Perhaps her true feelings for her daughter-in-law—resentment, jealousy, or anger—are suggested in this nebulous term *twick,* which sounds like both a compliment and an insult. These comments, made in ignorance, illustrate the lack of communication skill below the surface of the humor. Tyler has said that her novels employ a "blend of laughter and tears" because "that's what real life consists of," and by juxtaposing the theme of miscommunication with the comic dialogue, Tyler magnifies truths on and below the surface.[14]

Realistic, significant, and humorous, southern dialogue is much more than conversation. People use language to convey intent, feelings, and needs; unfortunately, language many times fails them. When this happens, humor often lends a voice to what might otherwise not be said. As Regina Barreca explains, "Laughing together is as close as you can get to a hug without touching."[15] Perhaps, then, even if language fails, laughter will provide the needed connection.

An intimate and confessional tone is not the only characteristic contemporary women novelists share with Twain. Following in his tradition, women writers are creating what Hobson terms "contemporary Huck Finns"—characters who, through a variety of experiences, come to a better understanding of who they are and what they believe.[16] The *Bildungsroman* is perhaps the most common mode in recent southern fiction by women (the prefix *Bildung* meaning "education," "development," or "formation"), a term used to describe a novel about the development of a char-

13. Anne Tyler, *Breathing Lessons* (1988; rpr. New York, 1989), 199.
14. Tyler, quoted in Alice Hall Petry, *Understanding Anne Tyler* (Columbia, S.C., 1990), 6.
15. Barreca, *They Used to Call Me Snow White,* 105.
16. Hobson, *Southern Writer,* 77.

acter, usually but not always an adolescent. Sam Hughes in Mason's *In Country*, Jo Spencer in McCorkle's *The Cheer Leader*, Lucy Odom in Humphreys' *Rich in Love*, Bone Boatwright in Allison's *Bastard out of Carolina*, Crystal Spangler in Smith's *Black Mountain Breakdown*, Justin Stokes in Godwin's *The Finishing School*, Molly Bolt in Brown's *Rubyfruit Jungle*, Clay-Lee Calvert in Bosworth's *Almost Innocent*, Ginny Babcock in Alther's *Kinflicks*, Taylor Greer in Kingsolver's *The Bean Trees*, and the title characters in both *Ellen Foster* by Gibbons and *Clover* by Sanders, are just some of the characters in novels chronicling the adolescence of southern girls who eventually come to a better understanding of their identities, as well as of the roles they play in family and community.

Many of these novels share other important links to Twain's novel, one of which is first-person narration. Pascal Covici, Jr., notes the significance of using a naïve narrator and its relationship to humor: "The humor of naiveté is a tricky business to talk about, because, in Freud's terms, naiveté becomes wit the moment it is only pretended. Rather than being diminished by a narrator who does not know he or she is funny, the comedy is heightened for just that reason. In using this point of view, writers must be especially careful to separate themselves from the protagonists, a feat that helped make Twain's novel so successful. Covici remarks that even when events "are intrinsically far from funny," humor arises from this separation: "The division between Twain and Huck leads the reader to accept the human condition as Huck does, while lamenting abuses and perversions along with Twain. The balance is everything. Twain's art suspends the reader between outrage and sympathy. . . . The uneducated speaker is not simply a boor to be ridiculed; he is worth taking seriously, just as his clear vision— reflected through his language—is worth attention."[17]

A novel that successfully incorporates this balancing is *Bastard out of Carolina*, in which a poor girl, Bone, tells her story of violence, abuse, and eventual abandonment by a mother who chooses to leave with the man who has sexually abused her daughter. The balance "between outrage and sympathy" is partly accomplished by Allison's inclusion of Bone's naïve sense of humor, especially when it is contrasted with her mother's adult, keen humor. A novel about a young girl growing up as a bastard holds possibilities for tragedy, yet Allison turns the situation into a comic one instead. Bone's mother, Anney, is furious that her daughter's birth certificate lists Bone as a bastard, and so she makes annual trips to the courthouse for a new certificate, claiming the old one had been lost or torn. Each year, the new one is printed with the word "Illegitimate" on it until Anney becomes

17. Covici, *Mark Twain's Humor*, 90, 47.

the town joke, and the clerk admits to her, "By now, they look forward to you coming in."[18]

Rather than becoming bitter, Bone reports, Anney learns the value of humor: "There was only one way to fight off the pity and hatefulness. Mama learned to laugh with them, before they could laugh at her, and to do it so well no one could be sure what she really thought or felt." When people tease Anney about the certificate and ask where she keeps it, she uses defensive humor. " 'Under the sink with all the other trash,' she'd shoot back, giving them a glance so sharp they'd think twice before trying to tease her again." Eventually, the courthouse holding the official certificate burns down, leaving no proof that Bone is illegitimate. When Anney's sister, Ruth, calls her with the news, Anney is already standing over the kitchen sink with a match in her hand. When Ruth asks her if she has heard of the fire, Anney replies, "The only fire I got going here is the one burning up all these useless papers" (*BC,* 10–16).

This act, however, does not help Bone establish who she is; it only eliminates one possibility. To define herself, she must first do what Joan Schultz terms "orphaning," a common technique in the contemporary southern novel and a third link to Huck Finn:

> A substantial—and at first glance, surprising—number of women in novels and short stories of Southern women authors "orphan" themselves. . . . In doing so, they signal themselves as resisting, refusing, or rejecting the kind of family identity, family roles, and family ties with the past or the present considered so vital to the Southern way of life, sought after or lamented with such vigor and obsessiveness by male figures in Southern literature, and treated as the central response by male critics. . . . Frequently their female characters suggest by their words or actions that they prefer to risk solitariness, exclusion, estrangement, even isolation; that they prefer deracination—or even death—to absorption in the family of the past or present.[19]

For female characters, this process is often related to separation from patriarchal society. Also, this "self-orphaning" is often handled humorously, as in Bone's orphaning, which is retold by her Aunt Alma. In Bone's last encounter with her biological father, when she is eight days old, she symbolically and scatologically rejects him as a parent: "That boy was scared shitless, holding you in hands stained dark green where he'd been painting his

18. Dorothy Allison, *Bastard out of Carolina* (New York, 1992), 9.
19. Joan Schultz, "Orphaning as Resistance," in *Female Tradition,* ed. Manning, 92.

daddy's flatbed truck. You just looked at him with your black Indian eyes like he wasn't nothing but a servant, lifting you up for some air or something. Then you let loose and pissed a pailful all down his sleeves, the front of his shirt, and right down his pants halfway to his knees! You peed all over the son of a bitch!" (*BC,* 25).

Much as Huck Finn orphans himself by staging his own death, thereby separating his identity from his father's before leaving on his river trip with Jim, Bone initially separates herself from seemingly destructive familial alliances, first from her father and eventually from her mother. These separations leave her free to pursue a new direction in her attempts to define herself—perhaps "to light out for the territory" figuratively—a process that is begun in the last few paragraphs of the novel. When Anney leaves Bone in the care of her Aunt Raylene, she gives Bone only one thing: a new copy of her birth certificate. Where the word "Illegitimate" had been, the certificate is "blank, unmarked, unstamped," leaving Bone to determine her own identity. Ironically, in the final paragraph, Bone decides: "I was already who I was going to be . . . someone like [Aunt Raylene], like Mama, a Boatwright woman." With the decision left to her, Bone chooses to emulate the strong women in her family. She seeks to develop their positive traits as well as accept their weaknesses as she sees them: "strong . . . hungry for love . . . desperate, determined, and ashamed" (*BC,* 309).

Bone's initial orphaning and eventual acceptance of her heritage follows closely Joseph Campbell's cyclical pattern of the hero's development established in his book *The Hero with a Thousand Faces*—separation, initiation, and return. Significant differences, however, can be found in Allison's novel, including the fact that Bone's journey is psychological rather than physical. Whereas Campbell's study of the hero/quest deals strictly with male heroes of high status, class, and race, Bone represents the contemporary hero as put forth in the feminist answer to Campbell's work, *The Female Hero in American and British Literature,* by Carol Pearson and Katherine Pope. According to Pearson and Pope, female heroes, like males, begin their journeys as orphans, but the female's journey is usually internal, and the dragons she fights are those found in patriarchal society. Because these women challenge societal authority, their victories are often secret and personal, but heroic nonetheless. Most important, however, Pearson and Pope point out that the female hero "masters the world by understanding it, not by dominating, controlling, or owning the world or other people," an observation that complements the theory that women use humor to understand and unite rather than to dominate and control.[20]

20. Carol Pearson and Katherine Pope, *The Female Hero in American Literature* (New York, 1981), 5.

Bone's journey is private and quiet. One of her dragons is her stepfather, representative of the patriarchy that overpowers her both physically and emotionally. With a blank birth certificate in front of her, Bone has the opportunity to erase her heritage, but she chooses instead to stay with her Aunt Raylene. This act and this attitude set her apart from male heroes. Pearson and Pope argue that whereas male heroes are portrayed as "antiheroes in a hopeless and meaningless world," women protagonists, like Bone, are "increasingly hopeful, sloughing off the victim role to reveal their true, powerful, and heroic identities."[21] And although this novel hardly ends with unqualified happiness and at times is heart-wrenching, it does conclude with a sense of affirmation and hope for Bone's future. Readers see enough of Bone to believe that she will survive and be stronger because of her challenging beginnings and, like Faulkner's best characters, will not merely endure but prevail.

Southern fiction by women abounds with orphans like Bone, some self-made and some actual, many of whom are forced to leave their environment and change their names in order to survive, unlike Bone, who stays, keeps her name, and chooses her identity. Characters who are female, children, and orphans comprise one of the least powerful groups in society, and yet their laughter claims authority first by defying convention and then by subverting it. Humor strips away power from authority figures by thwarting expectations, and orphans are the freest to do so. With few restrictions and little social status, an orphan is liberated. Having once rejected the norms of society, an orphan can more easily continue to break the rules, often without knowing it and often with impunity—especially if that orphan is a naïve child.

After both her parents die, Kaye Gibbons' title character in *Ellen Foster* is passed from home to home. Another naïve first-person protagonist, Ellen is full of humorous insights into her life, such as her memory of her mother, who, she reports, had "romantic fever." In one scene, holding a woman's baby on the way to her own mother's funeral, Ellen hears the woman comment on the beautiful day, and Ellen thinks, "My mama is dead in the church, my daddy is a monster, your girl is probably going to pee on me before this ride is over and that is all you can find to say" (*EF,* 3, 16). Her realistic view of her predicament, told in such an ironic tone, reveals a sharp perception below the narration, more so than she realizes, just as Huck never recognizes the truth he speaks. More important, though, Ellen is also excused from obeying cultural and social rules. She is allowed to say and do what others would not, simply because she lacks any social status and, without realizing it, assumes control of her life and identity.

21. *Ibid.,* 13.

As Huck Finn does several times in Twain's novel, Ellen creates a new name for herself, calling herself Ellen "Foster" because she hears a social worker say that she will soon be going to the "foster" home. In her struggles to put the pain of her real family and identity behind her, Ellen sees the necessity for a new name. She says: "That may not be the name God or my mama gave me but that is my name now. Ellen Foster. My old family wore the other name out. . . . That one is fresh. Foster" (*EF,* 88). Just as Bone feels it is important to reject her father before moving toward a self-definition, Ellen rejects her father's name for the same reason. The act of naming oneself is empowering, especially for women, since children are traditionally named by their fathers and women take the name of their husbands. By changing her name, a woman takes control of her identity, separating herself from her patriarchal lineage. Because Ellen renames herself naïvely, readers laugh, and it is just this kind of laughter that is subversive. With this simple act, Ellen has questioned, exposed, and mocked the patriarchal structure.

Symbolically, taking a new name is also important because it signals beginning a new life, not just detaching oneself from the life left behind. In Barbara Kingsolver's *The Bean Trees,* the protagonist leaves rural Kentucky and heads west, hoping to escape the fate of many of her friends: early marriage, pregnancy, and a life sentence of poverty and ignorance. She does not know who her father is, and her mother encourages her to leave, making her an orphan, at least symbolically. She reveals her sure sense of humor in her method for choosing a new name:

> The first [promise] was that I would get myself a new name. I wasn't crazy about anything I had been called up to that point in life, and this seemed like the time to make a clean break. I didn't have any special name in mind, but just wanted a change. The more I thought about it, the more it seemed to me that a name is not something a person really has the right to pick out, but is something you're provided with more or less by chance. I decided to let the gas tank decide. Wherever it ran out, I'd look for a sign.
>
> I came pretty close to being named after Homer, Illinois, but kept pushing it. I kept my fingers crossed through Sidney, Sadorus, Cerro Gordo, Decatur, and Blue Mound, and coasted into Taylorville on the fumes. And so I am Taylor Greer. (*BT,* 11–12)

The orphan motif is further developed when Taylor becomes "mother" to an orphaned Native American baby whom she has to name. The messages sound clear: first, families do not have to be based on blood and may be better based on choice; and second, sometimes escape and "rebirth" are necessary for the survival of self. Most important, though, she chooses her own name and her daughter's name randomly. Whereas the traditional system for naming children and women maintains hierarchical order, a haphazard method challenges this system, showing it to be a fragile structure without substance. Like Dorothy in *The Wizard of Oz,* young girls who have been told to "pay no attention to the man behind the curtain" look anyway, discovering the male wizard is not so powerful after all; authority and power lie within themselves, waiting to be used.

Even some protagonists who are not actual orphans imagine for a time that they are, perhaps as a step in the distancing process described by Schultz and as an attempt to redefine themselves in terms separate from those of patriarchal society. Kate Burns, McCorkle's protagonist in *Ferris Beach,* hopes she is the "love child" of her wild and mysterious cousin, Angela, rather than the offspring of her own unexciting parents. Kate finally asks her mother for her birth certificate, ostensibly for a school report, and is disappointed when it is handed over without comment. The disappointment is mitigated, however, by her imaginative friend, Misty, who reasons: "Maybe she had it all planned. . . . I mean, she knew that sooner or later you'd ask questions, right? So you see she had this *fake* birth certificate all printed up and waiting in that drawer."[22] Refusing to accept her place as defined by her family and society, Kate holds out hope that she is an orphan. Such humor exposes the way society attempts to keep people in their places—sexually, racially, economically—and in defying that system, characters weaken it by refusing to believe in it or to support it. As long as Kate believes in her orphan status, she frees herself to make her own rules and to occupy any place in society.

In *The Cheer Leader,* however, McCorkle illustrates that not everyone would regard orphanhood as liberating. Some people depend on the rules of society because they crave the status and order that hierarchy provides. The protagonist, Jo Spencer, worries about her connection to her family, afraid that without a real family, she would lack a real identity. Jo explains that her fear of being an orphan stems from a story her brother had told her: "Bobby told me that he was the real child and that I had been left in the trashpile by some black people who did not want me" (*C,* 4). Unlike the glamor imagined by Kate in being a "love child," Jo's illusory orphaning makes her feel unloved and unwanted. But the novel is about a young woman without an identity and without the strength to develop one. As the title suggests, she sees herself as what she does, not who she is. She can-

22. Jill McCorkle, *Ferris Beach* (1990; rpr. New York, 1991), 78.

not survive without the hierarchical structure to define, support, and protect her. McCorkle illustrates the importance of appearance to Jo in a scene in which Jo tries to reassemble a family history whose significance is dependent upon her existence: "I just sat with the picture box and spread its contents all over the floor. Then I would go through one by one and try to put them in chronological order so that I could see myself, my history, the parts that I could not remember. One day I labeled all of those parts. I wrote B. J. (before Jo) in black magic marker . . . I put a neat circle around myself every time that I appeared. It seemed very important that all of that be done, even after my mother discovered my documentation and switched the hell out of me" (2).

Jo finds her identity through a link to her family because she lacks self-sufficiency and a vision of herself outside the structure of family and society. More often in contemporary southern fiction, however, female characters feel a need to flee that structure, especially in novels following the cyclical, picaresque pattern that allows at least a temporary escape. Typically, the picaresque novel includes a journey of some sort, away from familiar settings to new ones in which characters learn about themselves through a variety of adventures, similar to the separation stage Campbell identifies. As a fourth and final link to Huck Finn, female protagonists often leave home and the structure of society, learning about and defining themselves in the process. Unlike Huck, however, they sometimes return home, at least temporarily, to put the new knowledge to the test of the old life, again following Campbell's pattern of separation, initiation, and then return.

This cyclical pattern is clearly developed in two similarly structured comic novels: Doris Betts's *Heading West* and Anne Tyler's *Earthly Possessions*. Both novels involve women who feel trapped in their lives and who are kidnapped and taken away from their homes and families on a long journey, satirically illustrating the powerlessness of women to determine their own fates. Although both women want to escape on either a conscious or subconscious level, they are not allowed to make that decision; it is determined by men who are more concerned about their own escape. At some point in each novel, however, the protagonist stops playing the victim and begins looking at the experience as an adventure that teaches her about herself and her own previously hidden powers. The denouement in both novels finds the women returning home, one permanently and one temporarily, with newfound understanding about themselves as individuals and as members of a family. Most important, a sense of humor helps the women not only to survive the ordeal but also to see themselves and their families more clearly and realistically, to define new roles in the family structure.

The structure of these two novels differs significantly from the female

Bildungsromane discussed earlier. Traditionally, the structure of such novels is linear, following the chronological development of an adolescent. In *The Voyage In: Fictions of Female Developments,* however, a second pattern, used almost exclusively in female *Bildungsromane,* is identified. There is a "deferred maturation" or awakening that "may be compressed into brief epiphanic moments," occurring usually after women fail in "the fairy-tale expectation that they will marry and live 'happily every after.'"[23] Such is the case in both Betts's novel and Tyler's, one of which centers on an older, unmarried woman, and the other on an unhappy wife.

The protagonist of *Heading West,* Nancy Finch, is, according to Dorothy Scura, "a worthy addition to the gallery of American heroines," whose ranks include Hester Prynne, Catherine Barkley, Nicole Diver, and Caddie Compson. Scura sees Nancy as "the only one with a sense of humor." There is no debating that kidnapping is a serious subject, and Betts does not approach it lightly. Throughout the novel, the reader is always aware that Nancy's life is in danger, that her abductor, Dwayne, has a gun, and that her future lies in the hands of this unpredictable and deranged man. Nancy's sense of humor, however, is her strength, as Betts has explained: "I think of humor as fruit of character, usually a means of coping by said character." Betts endows Nancy with a comic sense even before the kidnapping, a useful trait in her work as a librarian: "Once a strange man had appeared in the library, unzipped his trousers, and laid out his penis on the edge of her desk—only to bolt when she made a move to staple it there."[24] Once Dwayne takes Nancy captive and begins to drive west with his hostage, this same gritty humor works as a survival technique.

Nancy has the added burden of menstruating on the journey, but the physical and emotional discomfort from this uniquely female ordeal does not deter her from her stoic determination to survive, nor does it have an impact on her humor. She imagines the wording of the all-points bulletin released by the police: "Be on the lookout for a man, dementia praecox, and a woman, premenstrual tension. Approach with caution" (*HW,* 31). Much of the humor in this passage comes from Nancy seeing herself as dangerous—because she is a woman, rather than in spite of it. Later in the novel, she imagines a newsflash: "Miss Nancy Finch of Gaza, North Carolina, taking the Grand Western Tour, when last seen was getting a headache from a mixture of eyestrain plus periodic female edema" (93). Nancy's wry

23. Elizabeth Abel, Marianne Hirsch, and Elizabeth Langland, eds., *The Voyage In: Fictions of Female Development* (Hanover, N.H., 1983), 12.

24. Dorothy M. Scura, "Doris Betts at Mid-Career: Her Voice and Her Art," in *Southern Women Writers,* ed. Inge, 139; Doris Betts to the author, December, 1993; Doris Betts, *Heading West* (New York, 1981), 198.

perspective allows her to step outside her situation and view its absurdity, a common strength in comic heroes and one that helps her maintain her courage, humor, and survival instinct.

During the flight westward, Nancy begins to view her family and her home in an ironic light. Rather than anticipate her rescue with happiness, she begins to see her former life as a dutiful spinster daughter and sister as simply another kind of imprisonment. One of the first indications of this changing attitude is her reaction to a newspaper report in which her family has described her as "medium height, medium weight, dark brown eyes and hair, no identifying marks, last wearing a blue dress, bites fingernails." Suddenly, she sees herself as her family sees her: common, colorless, nondescript. She looks at her hazel eyes in the mirror, touches her long fingernails, runs her fingers over various scars, and notes that she does not even own a blue dress. Realizing that her family does not know what she looks like, let alone who she is inside, Nancy discovers that her identity is unclear even to herself. From this point on, she starts to develop a new identity, beginning with the denial of her old one by orphaning herself. When a patrolman stops their car and looks in the window, "Nancy's hand with its long fingertips came forward and spread itself on the seatback in plain view" (*HW,* 66–68).

After convincing the policeman and herself that she is not the colorless woman in the newspaper description who bites her fingernails, Nancy takes full responsibility for herself at the moment Betts tells us "she had made the trip hers" (*HW,* 68). She has claimed as her own both the journey she is making with Dwayne and her journey through life. Her desire to disconnect from her family continues. She says she "yearned toward that amnesia. They'll wake me up here, tomorrow, and I'll be a woman from Sandia Pueblo with no relatives. Speaking in Tigua. I can start over with a clear conscience" (111).

After the moment of her self-orphaning, the journey westward becomes the means for Nancy to redefine herself through her own eyes as well as those of the world. Part of the problem with the world's perspective, however, is that society often has a misguided, skewed sense of reality. Several times in the novel, Nancy is unable to convince people that she has been kidnapped. When she argues with Dwayne about taking separate rooms at a hotel, and Dwayne threatens her, Nancy observes wryly that "nowhere in America was there a bellboy or waitress or gas attendant who could distinguish abduction from marriage or cared to try" (*HW,* 73). Later, when she manages to escape temporarily from Dwayne at a campground, she cannot convince another man that her story is real. Instead, he analyzes her tale from a position of omnipotent patriarchy, telling her that she has invented this fantasy to compensate for an uneventful life, that Dwayne represents Satan in the fantasy, and that her sexual fears of rape are really repressed desires to lose her virginity. Again, she realizes she must take responsibility for herself and her fate: "For years she had dreamed of a different life, *any* life; this substitute now sounded so implausible no one would rescue her from this one, either" (150–51).

Because Nancy knows she cannot develop a new self while under the control of her family or a kidnapper, she eventually escapes into the Grand Canyon, where she is pursued by Dwayne. At the end of her ordeal, the power of humor—laughter, specifically—saves her. Standing face to face with her abductor, his gun aimed at her head, Nancy knows that only she has ultimate control over her life—whether she lives or dies. She laughs at him while he orders her to stop: "But no other threats were now large enough to reinforce his order. Nancy could not keep from laughing, her lungs so dry she was afraid of sounding like a mockery of him: *huh-huh! huh-huh!* She, who should be saying the Twenty-third Psalm, was in a reactive fit as persistent as hiccups" (*HW,* 207).

Laughter claims its own authority, just as rage does, and this unsolicited laughter empowers Nancy, reducing Dwayne's authority so significantly that his phallic gun becomes useless in the traditional sense. Instead of shooting her, he prepares to hit her with the gun, but at this moment, Betts writes, "Nancy changed in an instant" (*HW,* 207). She throws a rock at him, he jerks aside and stumbles, stepping awkwardly over the edge into the canyon. This darkly comic scene filled with aggressive and defiant laughter shows the kind of humor Betts has said she prefers to use: "the half-humorous, half-sardonic comment that circumstance seems to WRING out of a fuller character, one who is capable of laughing at herself."[25] Certainly, this situation wrings humor out of Nancy, forcing her to laugh not only at herself but also at Dwayne and the subjugation he represents. Laughter has saved her, changed her, and helped her redefine Nancy Finch as active, independent, and strong.

Nancy returns home, not sure how this new self will fit with the old perceptions her family has of her. It is clear from her encounter with her family that she is different, so different that it seems unlikely she will stay with them for very long. Betts writes that although the novel "ends with Nancy not having gotten very far on the American pursuit of happiness . . . she HAS acquired cheerfulness. I think that's what I mean by humor that has

---

25. Doris Betts to the author, December, 1993.

an edge, a wryness. It knows that the abyss runs right down Main Street, but agrees with our southern grandmas: 'you might as well laugh as cry.' "[26]

Choosing to laugh rather than to cry is also what helps Charlotte Emory to survive emotionally in Tyler's *Earthly Possessions.* Published four years before *Heading West,* this novel also traces the journey of a kidnapped woman, this time heading south instead of west. Like Nancy, Charlotte is unhappy with her mundane life, and although she plots for years to leave her preacher husband and his brothers, she has been unable to do so, mired as she is in passivity. She admits, "I would rather die than make any sort of disturbance."[27] Ironically, when Charlotte finally gets the nerve to leave, she does not get the chance. While withdrawing money from the bank for her "escape," she is taken hostage by a bank robber and is forced to leave, unable to tell her family that she is leaving by her own volition.

Interposed between chapters about the kidnapping are chapters in which Charlotte describes her life up until the moment she is abducted. In one passage, Charlotte describes her mistaken belief that she is an orphan. Although Charlotte's mother denies the story before she dies, she tells her young daughter that there had been a mix-up at the hospital and she had been given the wrong baby. It is clear where Charlotte gets her passivity, for her mother's response to being given the "wrong child" reveals the same trait: "Why! I thought. *This* is not mine! But I was still so surprised, you see, and besides didn't want to make trouble. I took what they gave me" (*EP,* 15).

Like many of the orphans in contemporary southern literature, Charlotte has ambivalent feelings about the experience: "These were my two main worries when I was a child: one was that I was not their true daughter, and would be sent away. The other was that I *was* their true daughter and would never, ever manage to escape to the outside world" (*EP,* 17). The humor shown here about a serious issue expresses Charlotte's real fear: being trapped in a situation—any situation. What she finds as a hostage is no different from her experience at home in Clarion. Growing up, she defines home as a place where she is "trapped, no escape" (62). She sees marriage and her husband's church as claustrophobic: "They were keeping me here forever, all the long, slow days of my life" (96). When she finally leaves, it is as a hostage in a stolen car that feels as if it "could smother a person" (47). In a humorous exchange with Jake, her kidnapper-turned-confidant, she even compares her marriage to the car:

26. *Ibid.*
27. Anne Tyler, *Earthly Possessions* (1977; rpr. New York, 1984), 20.

"If you like," he said, "you can sleep in the back tonight. I ain't sleeping anyhow. I plan to just sit here and go crazy."

"Okay."

"I don't see how you stand this," he said.

"You forget," I told him, "I've been married." (110–11)

Although she is taken by force, at first Charlotte thinks of the journey as a positive experience, a way to escape: "I sank into a seat and felt suddenly light-hearted, as if I were expecting something. As if I were going on a *trip*, really" (9). She imagines sending a postcard to her husband, Saul: "Having wonderful time, moving on at last, love to all" (57).

The euphoria of "escape" is shortlived, however, as Charlotte comes to understand that imprisonment is linked to powerlessness, not to geography. She notices some of the same things Nancy Finch does, such as that no one questions a man's right to force a woman to do what he wants. The woman who sells them bus tickets, numerous waitresses, and other travelers all ignore Charlotte's pathetic attempts to draw attention to her predicament. Finally, she concludes that there will be no external help for her and, like Nancy, that she must take her fate in her own hands. Taking control of her life is a new experience for Charlotte, who had turned over all power to Saul when she married him: "All I had to do was give myself up. Easy. I let him lead me. I agreed to everything" (*EP,* 90). Similarly, on finding that no one would help her escape from Jake, she initially surrenders her fate to him: "I felt comforted. All I had to do was lift the cup, which was warm and heavy and solid. Everything else had been seen to. I was so well taken care of" (87). Through her journey south with Jake and her journey backward in memory, though, Charlotte learns enough about herself first to request and then to demand autonomy.

Slowly, she begins to realize she is as powerful as Jake, an equality symbolized by the "identical white shirts" they are wearing under the layers of clothing they shed as they drive south (*EP,* 107). She also remembers a conversation she had once with her brother-in-law, Amos, who describes a strong Charlotte she has not acknowledged. He tells her: "I didn't understand you. Now I see everyone grabbing for pieces of you, and still you're never diminished. Clutching on your skirts and they don't even slow you down. . . . You sail through this house like a moon, you're strong enough for all of them" (195).

The new self-definition developed by Charlotte through her journeys, internal and external, leads to her final confrontation with Jake, when she calmly and decisively tells him she is going home. The situation is a reversal of their first encounter: Charlotte and Jake go to another bank to cash a check, but this time she thinks, "I knew better by now than to count on other people for help." Charlotte controls this situation now because she knows her own strength, and Jake acknowledges that strength by asking her to stay: "Charlotte, but . . . see, I can't quite manage without you just yet. Understand? . . . You act like you take it all in stride, like this is the way life really does tend to turn out. You mostly wear this little smile" (*EP*, 217–19). Significantly, he describes Charlotte as smiling, an indication of her endurance, her strength, her humor, and a self-awareness of all three.

Unlike Nancy Finch, who returns home to find that her family still cannot see who she was and who she has become, and so will probably leave again, Charlotte Emory goes home seemingly to stay, empowered with a new vision of herself. Both women find strength they did not know they had, and neither will be able to approach her old life in the same way. Both women develop a new, constructive self-image, gaining autonomous strength from the experience and self-awareness that allows Charlotte to stay with her family but will most likely force Nancy to leave hers permanently. Most significantly, both women derive their strength from their ability to use humor in a potentially tragic situation, a humor that directs, comforts, and eventually saves them both.

chapter two

THE COMMUNION OF LAUGHTER:
HEALING AND UNIFYING COMEDY

A merry heart doeth good like a medicine:
but a broken spirit drieth the bones.

—PROVERBS 17:22

How dear the gift of laughter
in the face of the 8 hour day.

—PHILIP LEVINE

The power derived from the physical act of laughing has long been acknowledged by humor theorists. Laughing can bring not only a sense of
physical well-being but also emotional and psychological strength and autonomy as well as a feeling of unity with another individual or group. Unfortunately, not all theorists have seen this power as positive. Henri Bergson, for example, proposes that the function of laughter is to "intimidate by
humiliating" and suggests that laughter is a tool society uses to maintain the
status quo: "Laughter is, above all, a corrective. Being intended to humili-
ate, it must make a painful impression on the person against whom it is directed. By laughter, society avenges itself for the liberties taken with it. It
would fail in its object if it bore the stamp of sympathy or kindness."[1]

Freud, too, mentions the aggressive aspect of joke telling between two
people whose hostility is aimed at a third. The pleasure gained from laughing, according to Freud, is a release of emotional energy ordinarily repressed. Freud's conclusions have led to misunderstandings about women
and humor. Regina Barreca interprets Freud's ideas this way: "Freud and
his followers believed that women don't really need a sense of humor, because they have fewer strong feelings to repress, and this is where traditional
theories about humor fail in relationship to women. The argument runs
that women need to be naughty less because they are psychologically less
complex."[2] What early theorists like Freud failed to understand is that

1. Bergson, "Laughter," in *Comedy*, ed. Sypher, 188, 187.
2. Barreca, *They Used to Call Me Snow White*, 92.

women do not lack a sense of humor; they just find different things funny. What is more important, sometimes women use humor in ways men do not. Women recognize that laughter can be more than a weapon to use against others; it can also be a tool to bring people together.

One of the most basic powers of laughter is that of creating bonds and unity. Freud mentions the necessity for a partner in joke telling but theorizes that the ultimate motives for desiring laughter as a response are selfish: to reassure the teller of the success of the joke, to feel pleasure in the reaction of the hearer, and to "make up for the loss of pleasure owing to the joke's lack of novelty" for the teller. Bergson, too, discusses briefly the "complicity" of laughter as "a kind of secret freemasonry" with others who are laughing. Both Freud and Bergson, however, overlook the positive, unifying power of laughter, especially among women.[3]

Misconceptions about women and humor probably occur in part, as Barreca points out, because women tend to tell jokes only to other women; she claims it is "no surprise, then, that men have thought women have very little sense of humor. They have certainly been privy to very little of it. Women's humor was shut away from them." Traditionally, women have been taught through example and reinforcement to smile or to laugh at jokes told by men but to refrain from telling their own in mixed company. Social norms, according to psychologist Paul McGhee, dictate that "males should be the initiators of humor, while females should be responders." By not participating in joke telling, though, women can miss the positive effects of humor when coping with tragedy. Various theorists have described laughter as "saving therapy," "a weapon against defeat and despair," and our "most precious defense . . . against the inner horrors of guilt and despair."[4]

In medieval physiology, the body was believed to be controlled by four liquids called "humours": blood, phlegm, yellow bile, and black bile. "Bad humour" came from a lack of balance among the four, and a person was in "good humour" when no one humour dominated. Depending upon which humour was in oversupply, an imbalance caused physical, mental, or moral problems. Laughter, many believed, was the body's response to excess nervous tension, an attempt to restore the balance of humours. In other

3. Freud, *Jokes*, 191; Bergson, "Laughter," in *Comedy*, ed. Sypher, 53.

4. Barreca, *They Used to Call Me Snow White*, 104; Paul E. McGhee, "The Role of Laughter and Humor in Growing Up Female," in *Becoming Female: Perspectives on Development*, ed. Claire B. Kopp (New York, 1979), 183; Brom Weber, "The Mode of 'Black Humor,'" in *Comic Imagination*, ed. Rubin, 370; Ronald Wallace, *The Last Laugh: Form and Affirmation in the Contemporary American Comic Novel* (Columbia, Mo., 1979), 2; Covici, *Mark Twain's Humor*, vii.

words, laughter was believed to be a natural cure for bad humour/bad health. Although we no longer believe that the body and mind are controlled by four humours, we are at last beginning to acknowledge the power of "good humour." The past few decades have made great progress in clarifying the role of humor in both physical and psychological health, owing to the work of Norman Cousins, W. F. Fry, and J. Levine, and countless others.

Many women writers in the South have made good use of this knowledge. In novels that deal with tragic subjects, humor becomes the factor that saves characters, authors, and readers from sinking into despair, helping them find the balance between living with tragedy and being overwhelmed by it. In *Other Women,* Lisa Alther describes the role of humor in the early life of a woman who later becomes a nurse: "But her role in life was to help others feel better. Her parents used to come to the dinner table exhausted from their welfare work, and she'd tell every new joke she could think of, whatever her own prior mood. It had been worth it to watch them smile reluctantly, then laugh. As satisfying as watching the color return to patients' faces as you resuscitated them."[5]

But the power of laughter goes far beyond such physical healing; it also plays an important role in healing relationships and fostering unity among families and friends. Recognizing that there is strength in numbers, many women learn early to employ humor to form same-gender friendships, creating a unique form of communication based on mutual joys and sorrows, punctuated by laughter. Rita Mae Brown's Molly Bolt in *Rubyfruit Jungle* comments: "I decided to become the funniest person in the whole school. If someone makes you laugh you have to like her. I even made my teachers laugh. It worked." In another novel, Brown proposes that among females, laughter and communication are linked, especially in the South. When two southern women meet, Brown writes, there is "a joyous screaming and hugging known only to Southern women."[6] Women in the South seem to understand the communion of laughter, as a character in the same novel explains: "As we say in Runnymede, I've been up the road and I've been down the road. I learned I'd rather laugh than cry. Whenever possible I'll laugh. I also figure that other people have their fair share of pain, problems, and the heartbreak of psoriasis. If I have any compassion at all for them, I'll try to make them laugh too" (*B,* 123).

Laughter and emotional healing are often linked, as in Gail Godwin's

---

5. Lisa Alther, *Other Women* (1984; rpr. New York, 1985), 32.
6. Rita Mae Brown, *Rubyfruit Jungle* (1973; rpr. New York, 1988), 62; Brown, *Bingo* (1988; rpr. New York, 1989), 211.

The Odd Woman, in which laughter, with a little help from liquor, unites Jane Clifford and her mother, Kitty. Although their relationship had never been antagonistic, it had not been intimate or trusting either, ever since Kitty remarried and brought a new husband and daughter into Jane's teen-age world. As she grew older, Jane stopped expecting intimacy in the relationship, relying more on her grandmother, Edith, for advice and comfort. The novel begins with Edith's death and Jane's return home for the funeral, and Jane eventually finds herself alone with Kitty to sort through her grandmother's belongings.

To make the work go faster and be less emotionally draining, Jane and Kitty sip Edith's sherry. At first, their conversation dwells on their differences, Kitty expressing disappointment in the choices she has made in her life and Jane expressing anger and resentment over what she perceives as her mother's neglect. But as the afternoon wears on, the layers of anger begin to dissolve as laughter replaces resentment. Jane notices that in her mother, usually closed and distant with her, something "insurrectionary had certainly surfaced . . . and Jane giggled, delighted."[7] Descriptions of various kinds of laughter fill the following pages: As they read Edith's diary, the two are sent into a periodic "peal of giggles." When Kitty's husband, Ray, telephones and they realize they are drunk, the hilarity of the situation occurs to Kitty: "She caught Jane's eye. The two of them went into a paroxysm of giggles," which turns into "riotous laughter," and even as she begins to sober up, Kitty "still veered dangerously toward rebellion and hilarity." When Ray arrives to drive the two women home, Kitty tries to maintain self-control because he appears to her "mature, reproachful," but with one witty remark from Jane, "Kitty's façade of composure cracked and she hooted with laughter." After a few harsh words from Ray, however, Jane watches while "Kitty crumpled," returning to her former, unapproachable self (*TOW,* 179–82).

The door between mother and daughter, temporarily opened through laughter, closes again, but Jane will forever see her mother differently. She tells her mother that even though they had been drunk, they had "had [their] best conversation . . . in years" (*TOW,* 187). The significance of this scene is not that mother and daughter get drunk together, for sherry is only the catalyst for the more important event of the afternoon: laughter leading to connection. The release of inhibitions culminating with uncontrolled laughter bonds the two women. In addition, their unifying laughter temporarily excludes Ray, the authority figure, for nothing makes us laugh harder than someone telling us to stop. For a short time, laughter moves

---

7. Gail Godwin, *The Odd Woman* (1974; rpr. New York, 1985), 174.

Jane from her marginal position in the family—at least as she perceives it—to the center with her mother, and Jane and Kitty are able to reexperience the closeness they had not felt since before Kitty's marriage years before.

A somewhat different, though no less powerful, kind of bonding between mother and daughter is illustrated in a novel by Fannie Flagg. Walking home from the wrong bus stop, Daisy Fay's mother tries to avoid an oncoming car by running toward the curb, "but there wasn't even a curb on that side, just an embankment. She hit the side of it so hard that her high heels stuck in the mud and she bounced back out into the middle of the street. When she landed, her coat flew over her head and she skidded with her purse out in front of her."[8] All passersby can see is her alligator purse and silver fox coat; she appears to be an odd creature with "an alligator head on a fur body in the middle of the winter in Jackson, Mississippi." Although the scene is potentially tragic, Flagg unites mother and daughter through laughter, rather than separating them with anger. The daughter narrates: "Walking behind her the rest of the way home, I started to laugh and almost choked myself to death trying not to because I knew for sure she would kill me. I tried to pretend I was coughing. My face turned beet red and tears were streaming down my face. It's funny how when your life is in danger, you can't stop laughing, but when Momma turned around to beat me to death or worse, I was saved. She started to laugh. Then we both laughed so hard we had to sit down in the street and I ruined my mother-daughter dress" (*DF,* 23).

This scene is similar to the one in Godwin's novel in several ways. By laughing, Daisy Fay risks alienating her mother (and like Jane and Kitty, knowing she should not laugh makes it impossible not to). Rather than reacting as Ray did—as the authority figure—Daisy Fay's mother uses her own laughter to unite with rather than separate from her daughter. This bonding process for females may be an extension of Barreca's theory about the differences between male and female joke telling: "Where men hear something funny and want to 'top it' with one of their own stories, women hear a funny story and think 'Oh, thank God, that happened to you, too! It means I'm not crazy!'"[9] By seeing herself as her daughter sees her, Daisy Fay's mother is able to appreciate the absurdity of the scene.

In addition to breaking down boundaries, laughter can help define them as well. Traditionally, a woman—especially a mother—is stereotyped as someone on whom everyone else depends, often to the point of obscuring her identity as an individual, and part of a woman's growth may include

8. Fannie Flagg, *Daisy Fay and the Miracle Man* (1981; rpr. New York, 1992), 22.
9. Barreca, *They Used to Call Me Snow White,* 118.

learning to forgive others and herself for unreal expectations. By the end of Michael Lee West's *She Flew the Coop,* Vangie Nepper has lost her husband, first to his mistress and then to death, and has also lost her daughter to suicide. It is difficult to see this woman's situation as positive, and yet the novel is partly the story of Vangie's liberation from a domineering and deceitful husband, a loveless marriage, and a role of constant service that has buried her own identity. In the epilogue to West's novel, Vangie is slowly rebuilding her life. She is becoming more aware, more pragmatic, more autonomous. At first it appears her life has been destroyed when in fact she is on the verge of building a better one, the first life created by and for herself. The final paragraph describes a small plane which "drew out V's, one after the other, filling the sky," suggesting Vangie's name and identity, V for victory, and also the pattern created in the sky by migrating birds, forced to leave one place but moving toward a better one.[10] Most important, she hears *laughter,* "real or imagined, or something carried by the wind," rising up to remind her of the power of laughter in healing, in developing strength, and in progressing (*SF,* 390). Laughter gives female characters an alternative to madness, death, or marriage, the fates available to fictional women of earlier generations. Some contemporary authors show all three as possibilities a woman might consider or phases through which she might pass, as in West's novel, in which Vangie has to endure a bad marriage and the death of her depressed daughter before she can choose a more positive direction. And even though her future happiness is tenuous, still there is hope.

Even in a novel like Lee Smith's *Black Mountain Breakdown,* in which the protagonist, Crystal, suffers depression that eventually leads to a "paralyz[-ing of] herself," readers are not left without this hope.[11] Crystal has spent her life becoming what she thought she should be and what others expected: cheerleader, beauty queen, wife of a successful and wealthy politician. Ironically, her "breakdown" is one of the first things she has done that is truly of her own making. In the final paragraph, there is the sense that she is finally content: "And who knows what will happen in this world? Agnes reflects. Who knows what the future holds? . . . Why, Crystal might jump right up from that bed tomorrow and go off and get her Ph.D. or do something else crazy. She's just thirty-two now. . . . Or she might stay right here and atrophy to death. What Agnes really thinks, though, is that Crystal is happy, that she likes to have Agnes hold her hand and brush her hair, as out-

10. Michael Lee West, *She Flew the Coop* (New York, 1994), 390.
11. Lee Smith, *Black Mountain Breakdown* (1980; rpr. New York, 1991), 237.

side her window the seasons come and go and the colors change on the mountain" (*MB*, 239–40).

There is an atmosphere of peace in this passage, and an ironic, almost humorous tone; there is a sense that not everything has been decided and that possibilities remain in the seasons to come. Unlike earlier fiction—for example, Charlotte Perkins Gilman's "The Yellow Wallpaper," in which the woman's escape ends in madness—Crystal endures her mental breakdown, which, in time, could be a break*through* to a more fulfilling life. Also significant is that Crystal's breakdown is attended by her female friend Agnes, who, more than anyone else in Crystal's life, has been constant in love and humor, even in this seemingly bleak scene. More often than not, women find humor and strength through other women—a characteristic of women's humor that Nancy Walker has identified. She argues that often in women's comedy, there is a revelation that men are "nearly extraneous to the 'real' lives of women."[12] Such a declaration indeed disrupts social structure, as women's comedy tends to do.

In Josephine Humphreys' *Rich in Love,* this social disruption begins when Helen Odom leaves her husband "to start a second life." The residual effect of this act is that her seventeen-year-old daughter, Lucy, is left feeling abandoned and burdened with the care of her surprised and emotionally wounded father as well as her newly married and pregnant older sister and her husband, who descend upon the home in ironically named Mount Pleasant, South Carolina. Paralleling the breakdown of the family and its traditions is the destruction of the Old South and its replacement with an ostentatious and artificial New South, where names like "Seagull Shores" and "Gator Pond Estates," Lucy observes, are chosen as "memorials to what had been bulldozed into oblivion" (*RL*, 6). Like the developers, Helen clearly seems unbothered by the chaos her decision creates and the structure she disrupts, a common characteristic of female comic heroes. As Regina Barreca argues, in women's comedy, the humor is derived "not from the perpetuation of the familiar but from its destruction. This pleasure depends on surprises, disruptions, reversals, disunity and disharmony."[13] Many female characters do not mind disruption for the simple reason that patriarchal structure has rarely placed them in a position that has been satisfactory in the past; disorder is preferred over an order that subordinates them.

12. Walker, "*A Very Serious Thing*," 13.

13. Josephine Humphreys, *Rich in Love* (1987; rpr. New York, 1988), 18; Regina Barreca, *Untamed and Unabashed: Essays on Women and Humor in British Literature* (Detroit, 1994), 19.

This attitude is not shared, however, by Lucy, who equates stasis with contentment, order with happiness. Much of both the tragedy and the comedy in this novel result from Lucy's need for control and structure. The simplicity of the mother's farewell message, lacking in sentiment and written impersonally on a word processor, shocks Lucy's strong sense of propriety and her romantic sensibilities. She comments that "it might have been a note saying she was stepping out for a yoga class or a camellia show." Taking on the burden of protecting her father without his asking, Lucy writes by hand a substitute letter, falsely describing her mother as feeling "absolutely *adrift*" with "an emptiness at the heart of things." She ends the note with "All my love," forging the signature and rationalizing that the "essence of the message" is the same; she only makes it "more polite." But Lucy's attempts to maintain order actually create more chaos, leading to an ironic misunderstanding on her father's part because he claims the tone of the note is wrong; it "reads like a note that someone forced her to write." He determines, therefore, that it must be "a cry for help" (*RL,* 18–22). Because Lucy alters the businesslike tone of the letter, her father wastes months driving around the countryside searching for his wife, who he believes left against her will.

Lucy's actions are the result of her fears of change and of loss of control. Rather than adjusting to disorder, Lucy continues to maintain the illusion of order. She enjoys watching her miniature television set because, she says, the "ambiguity of the picture appealed to me. It was always open to interpretation." Lucy can ignore her lack of control over major events, such as her mother's departure, by taking control over minor things like television shows and household chores. She comments: "I owned the house, this hour of the morning. If I wanted to I could burn it down and everything in it, or I could fix breakfast. It was a moment of power and charity every morning, when I made the decision to cook" (*RL,* 38). Lucy's humor here serves as more than a simple joke. As the novel progresses, Lucy learns to give up control, starting with small things—like cooking—and moving on to bigger ones—like divorce—and this is one way she has of "trying out" how it would feel. Having power over others but choosing not to use it is something Lucy will not learn until the end of the book and beyond. She is still too frightened about change to consider letting other people make decisions that affect her, no matter what the situation. Early in the novel, she explains her philosophy about the connection between knowledge and power; she says, "If forced to pass on a recipe, it is a good idea to sabotage it by calling for some ingredient that shouldn't be in there. Keep your recipes to yourself, as you keep every valuable bit of knowledge, I said. Above all, keep yourself to yourself" (57–58).

Lucy spends most of her energy trying to protect others, believing only she has the power to hold the family together, not realizing that she must allow herself to heal from what she perceives as her mother's abandonment before she can help anyone else. She must put aside her romantic notions of her parents reuniting and cope with disruption and change—which includes accepting the new romantic interest in her father's life, Vera, a feisty woman who describes herself as "a survivor" (*RL,* 253). Lucy, too, must decide she can and will survive this family evolution.

When Lucy's older sister, Rae, has difficulty giving birth, Helen Odom returns. Lucy observes, "Tragedy, well-known for its convoluted methods, reunited the family" (*RL,* 249). What Lucy does not realize is that tragedy has brought them together only temporarily, and that humor will help her accept her mother's inevitable departure. Lucy tenaciously attempts to hold the family together during the brief reunion, refusing to give her father the car keys so he can visit Vera, but one last comic episode finally forces Lucy to realize that she cannot control her father's life or her mother's decisions. After hiding the car keys, Lucy goes to bed and dreams of a lawnmower bulldozing her beautiful countryside, hearing the words, "*And you will stop . . . and you will be as if you never were*" (255). Waking, she realizes she does not want to be left out of the progress of the world or her family, does not want to be left behind.

Awake, she still hears the mower from her dream and glances out the window in time to see her father and describe the scene she witnesses: "I saw him nearing the corner streetlamp, then taking the turn at full speed, in the direction of Vera Oxendine's house. He sat tall, almost noble, riding his Snapper lawn mower into the dark of the oaks along Bennett Street." Finally, Lucy is forced to accept that people must make their own life choices and that relationships change. At the end of the novel, she knows she can make plans only for herself, remarking, "But who knows what will happen? We'll have to wait and see" (*RL,* 255–61). Significantly, Lucy has stopped trying to plan, predict, and control life.

Although Lucy has achieved growth, Humphreys resists the traditional happy ending—that is, comedy that reinstates the hierarchical structure. The novel implies that the disruption in the Odom family will continue beyond the final page, as Lucy's parents pursue their new lives with no guarantees that they will find anything better than the one they shared. Typical of contemporary women's comedy, Humphreys celebrates female experience and choice, allowing Helen to abandon the rules and become Scarlett rather than Melanie. No promises are made for her happiness—only possibilities—but even a chance for a more fulfilling life was usually out of reach for fictional females of earlier generations. Helen Odom will not need to walk into the water as Edna Pontellier does in Chopin's *The Awakening* or protect herself in madness, as does Gilman's narrator in "The Yellow Wallpaper." Helen's "therapy" is choice.

Therapy of a slightly different sort is needed in Mason's *In Country,* also narrated by a seventeen-year-old girl, Sam Hughes, who comes to a knowledge and understanding of her father's death in Vietnam, which occurred shortly before she was born. Sam will lose her romantic illusions of war and, much like Lucy in *Rich in Love,* learn to relinquish control over the lives of others, specifically her uncle, Emmett, who is suffering numerous physical and emotional illnesses still haunting him from his own Vietnam experience.

The novel is set in another optimistically named small town—Hopewell, Kentucky. When Emmett returns there after the war to live with Sam and her mother, Irene, no one yet realizes the long-term effects of that war. Fact and fiction are often confused; ironically, the first war to be made "real"—because millions of Americans watched the day's battles on the evening news—is perhaps the first war Americans cannot accept as real, choosing instead to believe the vision of war presented in movies, television, and books. Fred Hobson notes that some of "the inhabitants of the small town in Mason's western Kentucky give up; most just absorb disappointment and carry on with gritty determination, finding some temporary pleasure in the mass culture around them." But temporary pleasure is not all that Sam and Emmett find in mass culture; they also find humor that leads to healing. One of the main motifs in this novel is the television comedy M★A★S★H, which Emmett and Sam watch several times a night in reruns, even memorizing many of the lines until Sam can recognize parodies of the show: " 'It's digging-in-the-ditch time,' said Emmett, when he brought his pickax up from the basement. Sam recognized the source of the line: Colonel Blake saying 'It's lonely-at-the-top time' once when he had to make a difficult decision."[14] Mason closely connects real life, especially the war, with pop culture—such as music and television—throughout this novel. A remark by Emmett explains why: "When you're in country [in Vietnam], there's so little connection to the World, but those songs—that was as close as we came to a real connection" (*IC,* 111).

The significance of the television program seems fairly obvious, at least superficially: both the program and Emmett's life concern the war, its disillusioning power, and its debilitating effect on mind and body. On a deeper level, however, the program, a combination of both tragedy and comedy,

---

14. Hobson, *The Southern Writer in the Postmodern World,* 13; Bobbie Ann Mason, *In Country* (1985; rpr. New York, 1989), 65.

becomes more real to Emmett and Sam than the actual war, for it is through a death on the show that Sam first feels the loss of her father: "Years ago, when Colonel Blake was killed, Sam was so shocked she went around stunned for days. She was only a child then, and his death on the program was more real to her than the death of her own father. Even on the repeats, it was unsettling. Each time she saw that episode, it grew clearer that her father had been killed in a war. She had always taken his death for granted, but the reality of it took hold gradually" (*IC*, 25).

One of the most humorous recurring jokes on M★A★S★H is Klinger's attempts to get released from the army, dishonorably, by dressing as a woman. Seventeen years after Vietnam, Emmett borrows Klinger's tactic—"wearing a long, thin Indian-print skirt with elephants and peacocks on it"—as his own cry to be released from the pains of the war. Although everyone pretends the situation is a joke, Emmett's actions are very serious. Mason describes him while he is modeling the skirt as wearing "a gleeful expression that said he had gotten away with murder" (*IC*, 26–27), and certainly, by killing the enemy as part of a soldier's duty, Emmett feels he has. In addition, by mocking military rules, Emmett signals his refusal to participate in the system, and by wearing a dress, he challenges what society has deemed normal and sane, significantly disguising himself as a woman—a person who would not have been forced to go to war at all.

After seventeen years of joking and teasing, though, Sam and Emmett have not completely healed, and they both begin to see that on "M★A★S★H sometimes, things were too simple" (*IC*, 83). The final episode of M★A★S★H should end the Korean War for the program's characters but through reruns, the characters relive it, just as Emmett relives the Vietnam War; the war is in the past but never past. Sam hopes that Emmett will "come out with some suppressed memories of events as dramatic as that one that caused Hawkeye to crack up in the final episode of M★A★S★H. But nothing came." Instead, Emmett finally realizes that his experience "was completely different. It really happened" (222–23).

The final episode in the novel is a pilgrimage by Emmett, Sam, and Sam's paternal grandmother, Mamaw, to the Vietnam War Memorial. Unlike Sam and Emmett, who are working toward a significant understanding and acceptance of the war, Mamaw lacks any real understanding of her son's death, as is evidenced by the fact that she is more concerned with strangers who "might see up [her] dress" than in climbing a stepladder to touch her son's engraved name on the memorial. For Sam and Emmett, the trip culminates the healing begun with the comedy of M★A★S★H. Mason illustrates the power of fiction one final time when Sam finds a soldier's name that is the same as hers—"SAM A HUGHES"—and she feels the losses of the war as a universal loss of self, "as though all the names in America have been used to decorate this wall" (*IC*, 243–45). Fiction has once again helped her understand and accept reality.

Healing after the loss of a loved one is also a major theme in the novels of Anne Tyler, several of which begin immediately following a death. *The Clock Winder* concerns newly widowed Mrs. Emerson, who is adjusting to her new life and looking for someone to take care of the details formerly attended to by her husband; symbolically, she needs someone to wind all the clocks in the house. Tyler describes Mrs. Emerson as "not a stupid woman, but she was used to being taken care of," ironically giving her the last name of the writer most associated with self-reliance.[15] Mrs. Emerson finds the answer to her problem in the person of Elizabeth Abbott, a college dropout impulsively turned handywoman. As the novel begins, Elizabeth, like Mrs. Emerson, admits she craves order and direction in her life, acknowledging "there was something steady and comforting about printed instructions," but it is Elizabeth's nontraditional way of creating order and her sense of humor that help heal not only Mrs. Emerson but also her grown children and Elizabeth herself (*CW*, 77). Much like Lucy in *Rich in Love*, Tyler's two women characters learn to abandon the traditional, patriarchal order in which they have lived all their lives—with its ticking clocks and its specified roles for women—and instead discover the freedom and power in a life that includes flexibility, risk, and individual growth.

Although Elizabeth has no experience in home repair work and has a history of clumsiness, this new opportunity in a traditionally male job changes her reputation and the direction of her life: "From the day that Elizabeth first climbed those porch steps, a born fumbler and crasher of precious objects, she had possessed miraculous repairing powers" (*CW*, 70). Elizabeth's "repairing powers" refer not just to porches, rain gutters, and wobbly table legs but to human beings as well. At first, however, she refuses to accept responsibility for people as well as things, not wanting to "change someone else's affairs around" (55). Little by little, though, Elizabeth becomes a new kind of clock winder in relationships as well as in domestic chores.

A second death occurs when Timothy Emerson, enamored with Elizabeth, becomes jealous of her friendship with his brother Matthew. Timothy locks her in his apartment bedroom, demanding that she cancel a date with Matthew. Eternally optimistic, Elizabeth tries to relax and "see some humor in the situation." She attempts to joke her way out of the conflict by

15. Anne Tyler, *The Clock Winder* (1972; rpr. New York, 1983), 6.

making expensive long-distance phone calls from the bedroom, telling the operator, loudly enough for Timothy to hear, "Person-to-person. First class. Any *other* charges you can think of." When the door is finally opened, Elizabeth finds Timothy pointing a gun at himself. Again, Elizabeth uses humor, sure "he would laugh. Didn't he always laugh?" But when she eventually lunges for the gun, it discharges, killing him (*CW,* 88–94). Suddenly, the family has another death to cope with. Elizabeth, feeling guilty about her part in the debacle, returns to her parents' home, where she is considered by her family—and by herself—a clumsy, undirected failure.

The Emersons' need for Elizabeth's strength and humor does not end with Timothy's death. Another emotionally unstable brother, Andrew, holds Elizabeth responsible for the tragedy, and he writes threatening letters to her, describing his revenge in detail. After receiving numerous letters from him, Elizabeth once again uses humor in a letter she writes to end a potentially tragic event: *"Lay off the letters, I'm getting tired of them. If I'm not left alone after this I'll see that you aren't either, ever again. I'll fill out your address on all the magazine coupons I come across. I'll sign you up with the Avon lady and the Tupperware people. I'll get you listed with every charity and insurance agency and Mormon missionary between here and Canada, I'll put you down for catalog calls at Sears Roebuck and Montgomery Ward. When they phone you in the dead of night to tell you about their white sales, think of me, Andrew"* (*CW,* 161). This time the humor works, temporarily at least, and Elizabeth diverts tragedy. Eventually, Elizabeth returns to the Emerson household when Mrs. Emerson suffers a stroke, becoming the ultimate healer of body, mind, and family: "Putting on the Band-Aids" (250). This time, things are different because the family grants her total control, trusting in her "repairing powers." She is even given an absurd new name to represent her new status in the household, "Gillespie," created from Mrs. Emerson's jumbled attempt to pronounce Elizabeth's name after her stroke. Elizabeth does not mind the new name because it evokes images of "someone effective and managerial who was summoned by her last name" (much as men sometimes are) and represents the strength and authority she has developed in a still male-dominated world (244–45).

One last time, Elizabeth is faced with tragedy on an afternoon when Andrew confronts her with a gun, this time pointed at her. Her first inclination, as before, is "to laugh," but afraid that humor will be the catalyst for yet another disaster, she chooses not to. Her previous experiences have made her fear that laughter will "set explosions off." She remains calm, her demeanor serious, but Andrew shoots her in the shoulder anyway. Wounded slightly and lying on the grass, Elizabeth gives in to her initial inclination: "When Matthew reached her she was laughing. He thought she was having hysterics" (*CW,* 251–53). By describing Elizabeth's laughter as "having hysterics," Tyler denotes both the loss of control in the modern sense of the word and the historical "hysteria," an exclusively female disease believed to be caused by a disturbance in the womb. With this laughter, Elizabeth has denied Andrew's power both as her employer and as a man. The act actually frees her and moves her from a marginal position to one of centered authority.

The first indication of this reversal of roles is Andrew's immediate response to her "hysteria"; he changes from being aggressive and violent to being penitent and worried, acknowledging the shift in power. The final section of Tyler's novel, set years later, shows a different Elizabeth. She is married to Matthew and is still the official clock winder for the Emersons, now by her own choice and on her own terms. The ultimate scene is absurd, humorous, and chaotic, set during a year of locust infestation. Like the people Elizabeth cares for, the locusts seem unpredictable, uncontrollable, and driven by instinct, but throughout the mayhem, she maintains life on her schedule as the "juggler of supplies, obtaining and distributing all her family needed" (*CW,* 281). She has as much or more responsibility as before but has learned to relax, laugh, and let tragedy and comedy come as they will, trusting in her "repairing powers." Thus both Elizabeth's and Mrs. Emerson's lives are ordered in a different way than before. Their clocks tick to a new rhythm that both empowers and frees them.

The power to repair damage both physical and emotional is a motif running through Kaye Gibbons' *Charms for the Easy Life* as well. Indeed, one of the three main woman characters is a self-proclaimed healer and doctor. The novel concerns three generations of strong North Carolina women: Charlie Kate, a pragmatist and a healer; her romantic but stubborn daughter, Sophia; and Sophia's seventeen-year-old daughter, Margaret. Charlie Kate's skills as a doctor spring from practical experience, knowledge of herbs and other natural cures, and an innate understanding of human behavior along with an ability to tell people what they need to hear, and doing so with a keen sense of humor. In Charlie Kate, Gibbons has created an unconventional and memorable personality, bordering on eccentric, but full of wit, wisdom, and the strength to use both. When Sophia cautions Margaret to be careful or she will grow up abnormal like her grandmother, Margaret considers Charlie Kate's character and comes to this conclusion: "She wasn't normal in the sense of being like other people who worked in banks or stores, women with permanent waves and moisturized skin. But all the same, in the strangest sort of way, I considered her normal for herself.

It was normal for her to eat two cloves of raw garlic every morning, wear her late mother's seventy-five-year-old shoes, preserve the laces in linseed oil, and sit up all night laughing uproariously over *Tristram Shandy*."[16]

The family from which these women have sprung is in desperate need of someone like Charlie Kate—optimistic, strong, and nurturing—for they are obsessed with death, usually by suicide, and are a passionate clan who follow their hearts. Margaret explains the outcome of such passion: "That sort of hurling oneself at a desire is a family trait, and has made convicts, scholars, lovers, and dope fiends out of us from way back" (*EL,* 25). Into this family is born Charlie Kate, with a passion to heal rather than hurt. Her prescriptions are made up of home remedies and practical solutions to ailments; most of all, however, her cures are full of humor. To a young mother with a colicky baby, for example, she advises putting the child across her knees, "head down, looking at the floor," and the child will "go to sleep for nothing to look at but the floor. Anybody would" (61).

Her sexual instruction is graphic and practically unprecedented for the early part of this century. Concerning masturbation, she counsels boys: "Better to handle yourself than some girl. You do not know where she's been. You will not become a blind lunatic nor a rabid dog-boy. In fact, it may improve your attitude and render you less likely to get in scrapes at recess. You may be a more pleasant fellow all around for following your instincts in the PRIVACY of your room." To girls, her words are no less blunt: "She explained girls' bodies to them, corrected ruinous impressions created by the Baptists, and always ended her discussions with the same message: . . . 'Kiss all you want to. Kissing's fine, nothing more than uptown shopping on downtown business'" (*EL,* 39–40).

Included in her humorous advice is thinly disguised anger at a society that fears knowledge will lead to sin. Women often use comedy as social corrective—to expose weaknesses in that society—and this is the point at which humor becomes "dangerous" to those who claim authority. By refusing to play by society's rules by remaining silent, women like Charlie Kate threaten to disrupt social order, which is one reason why women's humor is often labeled irreverent and why characters like Charlie Kate are considered renegades and eccentrics. Such women dare to speak out on what society has marked as sacred themes: sex, religion, motherhood, marriage, and, especially in Charlie Kate's case, human relationships.

Not only does Charlie Kate help others, but she uses the same gifts of humor and practical thinking to help herself through her own crises. Early

16. Kaye Gibbons, *Charms for the Easy Life* (New York, 1993), 136.

in her life, Charlie Kate's husband deserts her, but he returns years later, determined to convince her to run away with him. Her pragmatic view of relationships, which includes the observation that her "shoestrings . . . have lasted years longer than most people can stand each other," (*EL,* 70) allows her to dismiss the sentimental attachments she once had to her husband, leave with him temporarily, and return alone with all his money, casually remarking to Sophia and Margaret, "I let him take what he wanted and then I took what I wanted" (75). By maintaining a sense of humor, Charlie Kate exposes traditional romance as debilitating and confining to women. Her actions are shocking because she rejects what men have believed is important to women—romance—for what a woman is supposed to find less valuable than love—money.

Charlie Kate's final accomplishment as a healer is not with a diseased body but with a confused spirit, that of her granddaughter, Margaret. Unsure of her future and afraid to leave the home and women she loves, Margaret flounders after high school. Aware of Margaret's fears but also of her talent for healing, Charlie Kate encourages her to stay home temporarily and get a job at a hospital for wounded soldiers. Certainly, Margaret has inherited her grandmother's insight into behavior as well as her sense of humor. Margaret takes it upon herself to edit, even rewrite, letters from soldiers to their homes and from home to soldiers, expressing what she believes they want and need to say. This is dangerous and disruptive, but it is also humorous and forgivable because her motives—to unite son and parents—are pure. Margaret knows she has "jumped off the roof of [her] sheltered life straight down into someone else's" and worries about how long she will have to intercept letters between mother and son: "I tried but could not shake the image of me at fifty, hiding behind a tree, waiting for her mailman to come, eventually being caught and dragged off to tell a true-crime tale of good intentions gone berserk that would horrify everyone in the world, except possibly my mother and grandmother, who would come to my trial and proudly testify, 'To have done it so well for so long—how grand!'" (*EL,* 167–68). Eventually, by following her grandmother's advice, Margaret does discover her calling as a healer and decides to attend medical school. From her experiences with her grandmother, Margaret learns not only the power of medicine but also "the power of a word"; more often than not, that word is spoken with a touch of humor (150).

At first, the theory that humor can be a means of healing and uniting does not seem to be supported in Tina McElroy Ansa's *Ugly Ways,* a novel about three sisters who are reunited at their mother's funeral. When the sisters meet at the airport, they play a game to see who can reveal the most shocking sexual exploit, such as Emily's confession that "I let a man I worked with stay at my house two nights once because he used the word 'juxtaposition' correctly in a sentence."[17] Such comic competition seems contrary to the theory that women use humor to connect while men use humor to "top" one another with a better story; but the competition, Ansa writes, is "more of a ritual" and has the effect of reconnecting the sisters by exposing their worst selves to each other, creating a fresh bond of intimacy and trust (*UW,* 7).

Throughout the novel, as in this first scene, laughter is the precursor to understanding and connection. Coming from a family that people in the town describe as having "'walking insanity' like other folks had 'walking pneumonia'" (*UW,* 11), the sisters use laughter as a defense against outsiders and as a link to one another: "The sisters laughed together so comfortably it sounded as if they were singing in harmony. They all three had felt at one time or another that the sound of them laughing together was their only line to sanity and safety. When all three of them laughed, in a department store or restaurant, the entire room turned to look for the source of the melodic merriment" (192). Since the word *comedy* originated with the Greek terms *komos* (to revel) and *aeidein* (to sing), it seems fitting that their laughter is described in musical terms. This suggests that although the sisters are different, they get along with one another, just as different notes on the scale can harmonize well. And by unifying the participants with laughter, "female" humor seems much closer to the original definition of comedy.

Since their youth, when their mother underwent a personality change, the sisters have clung to one another for support. Although there is a feminist message in this novel, there is also a protest against authority in general and against their mother, ironically named Mudear Lovejoy, in particular. As children, the Lovejoy sisters, Betty, Emily, and Annie Ruth, were terrified of their mother, a woman Betty compares to Medea and Emily confesses was *"the most powerful force on the face of the earth"* (*UW,* 132), lending support to the theory that women's humor attacks institutions and authorities rather than the defenseless and weak. As children, the sisters usually felt "as powerless as insects" (113) around her, praying to God "to help them, to protect them, to save them from their mother" (184). Because they all fear their unpredictably explosive mother, they soon discover "each other to be the best possible company" (186), forming a bond against her consuming control over their lives and strengthening that connection with laughter.

17. Tina McElroy Ansa, *Ugly Ways* (New York, 1993), 8.

Mudear raised her three daughters with a dark and misandrous sense of humor. As adults, her daughters reflect bleakly on her motto, "A man don't give a damn about you" (*UW,* 42), and remember comments that always disturbed them: Mudear often said "she was surprised more men aren't found murdered in their beds" (67), and "if the devil's wife had any sense she'd set his bed on fire while he was sleeping" (81). Their father, Ernest, admits he feels outnumbered, often fighting the urge to shout, " 'Women's taking over my house!' at the top of his lungs" (47). Ernest had made many mistakes early in his marriage, and Mudear gives him no chance to redeem himself; as Betty remembers, he was always treated as an outsider: "Whenever Poppa drove up in the driveway from work or an errand, one of the girls or Mudear would yell, 'Fire in the hole,' to warn the household that Poppa was on the premises. The girls didn't know at the time that the yell had been used originally as a warning in dynamite jobs, but when they each discovered its original meaning they had to chuckle" (128–29). Mudear uses laughter in this case to gain a position of power; Ernest fears this laughter because it signals his exclusion. While Mudear may seem heartless, laughter is the only means available to her to empower herself and her daughters.

To keep Mudear's character from becoming as destructive, cruel, and unsympathetic as Medea, Ansa employs various stylistic techniques and also endows Mudear with a sense of humor, savage at times but crackling with wit. First, through flashbacks, Ansa portrays Mudear as a victim in the early days of her marriage, a time when Mudear's only way to defy her husband was to burn dinner "until it was an okra holocaust" (*UW,* 130). Also, Ansa includes Mudear's own posthumous voice in occasional italicized chapters, narratives that tell her version of the story. In Mudear's chapters, it becomes clear that she views her daughters as weak and selfish, as drastically needing a strong, directive hand; in short, her daughters, she says, *"got ugly ways about 'em sometimes."* She lists the advantages she gave her daughters—manners, domestic skills, creativity, personal knowledge—and defends her firm hand: *"I didn't coddle 'em and cuddle 'em to death the way some mothers do. I pushed 'em out there to find out what they was best in. That's how you learn things, by getting on out there and living. They found their strengths by the best way anybody could: by living them"* (37). Ansa later adds, "Some respect was due her, Mudear felt, for not throwing herself down a flight of steps when she was pregnant with each one of them," a comment that softens, albeit ironically, Mudear's character and thinly disguises her rage in the cloaks of comedy (119).

According to Wylie Sypher, "Comedy reduces imposing figures," an idea clearly illustrated in the penultimate chapter of *Ugly Ways*.[18] Unable to free themselves from Mudear's influence even after her death, the three sisters visit the funeral home to have a final word with her. Recalling other great, blackly humorous funeral scenes in American literature, as in *Huckleberry Finn* and in Faulkner's *Sanctuary*, Ansa creates one of the most memorable such scenes in contemporary literature. The sisters fight with each other, getting heels and purse straps caught in the gurney holding the open casket, causing the gurney to collapse, the casket to tip over, and Mudear's body to pop "out of the satin-lined casket onto the floor like an ice cube out of a frosty tray [coming] to rest right at the girls' laps" (*UW,* 267).

The gruesome possibilities of the scene are mitigated by the visual slapstick, descriptions of Mudear as "stiff and straight as a little Popsicle," as well as the reaction of the daughters: they cry; they confess their pain and regrets; and they make a pact to go on with their lives, trying to get past the damage they believe Mudear caused. Acknowledging their own weaknesses, Betty goes on to address the corpse: "But now we gonna work on happy and peaceful and appreciative and joyful. . . . After being with you for forty years, we got being 'ranting, raving maniac' down pat. Now, we want to move on" (*UW,* 268–70). The women cry and mourn and wail, but Ansa writes that their teardrops "brought no healing relief for the girls" (271); instead, solace comes only from laughing together, which is "their own line to sanity and safety" (192). The sisters' tears are only a way to release the pain; their strength will come from the bond holding them together and the unifying laughter they share. Once again, women's comedy stops short of an unqualified happy ending. As in Humphreys' novel and others as well, only the possibility exists.

Much of the laughter in Ansa's novel originates with anger, a common thread in women's comedy. As Brenda Gross explains, "Women are getting to the point where we have all this rage, and it is personal, so we turn the rage into comedy." Often, humor is used by women as a way "to protest their condition," Nancy Walker notes, and "instead of meek acquiescence, the female humorist displays a fundamental understanding and rejection of her status and the absurdity of its premises," making it clear, through humor, that for women "a group other than themselves has made the rules by which they must live." Laughter seems to be the one response from women that men find threatening. The Texas journalist Molly Ivins relates this anecdote: "Margaret Atwood, the Canadian novelist, once asked a group of women at a university why they felt threatened by men. The women said

18. Sypher, *Comedy,* xv.

they were afraid of being beaten, raped, or killed by men. She then asked a group of men why they felt threatened by women. They said they were afraid women would laugh at them."[19]

More than any other southern novel, Alice Walker's *The Color Purple* exemplifies the power of laughter to defy authority, express anger, and unite women. The authority in the novel is twofold: male and white; therefore, the black women in this novel are surrounded by adversaries. Sexism and racism in the novel are both strong and vivid, and laughter is used to combat both. In her essay "Laughter as Feminine Power in *The Color Purple* and *A Question of Silence*," Judy Elsley explores the important role laughter plays in the two novels: it "acts as a catalyst . . . to self-empowerment"; it "dissipates the power of an oppressive culture"; and it bonds the women together, expressing "the women's growing sense of autonomy."[20]

The protagonist of Walker's novel, Celie, is much oppressed and intimidated, first by her stepfather and then by her husband, Albert, so much so that she is unable to call him by his first name, referring to him as "Mr. ———" instead. Through two strong and independent women, Shug and Sofia, Celie learns to laugh—and the laughter becomes an expression of her self-esteem and independence. The first time Celie sees Shug Avery is in a photograph Albert keeps of her, in which she is "grinning," "whirling and laughing."[21] Celie becomes entranced by Shug's self-assured image, partly because Albert has always been in love with Shug, and Celie is curious why he has loved her. Throughout the novel, Shug is shown laughing, a sign of her defiance of traditional roles society has failed to force her to play. Her attraction to Albert, she admits, is that "he make me laugh" (*CP*, 78), and when Shug eventually loses interest in him, it is for the opposite reason, as she explains to Celie: "Nobody dance like Albert when he was young . . . . And funny. Albert was so *funny*. He kept me laughing. How come he ain't funny no more? . . . How come he never hardly laugh? How come he don't dance? . . . What happen to the man I love?" (116). Shug underscores the need for people to laugh together in order to connect, no matter what gender. Without laughter, individuals grow apart or even fail to unite, as in the case of Celie and Albert.

Celie possesses a sense of humor, but she does not use it in front of Albert because, in her subservient role as wife, she views laughter as inappro-

19. Brenda Gross, "The Parallel Lives of Kathy and Mo," in *New Perspectives on Women and Comedy*, ed. Regina Barreca (Philadelphia, 1992), 95; Walker, *"A Very Serious Thing,"* x, 171, 13; Molly Ivins, *Molly Ivins Can't Say That, Can She?* (New York, 1991).

20. Judy Elsley, "Laughter as Feminine Power in *The Color Purple* and *A Question of Silence*," in *New Perspectives*, ed. Barreca, 193, 198.

21. Alice Walker, *The Color Purple* (1982; rpr. New York, 1983), 16.

priate and defiant. Her humor is evident only in her letters to her sister, Nettie, and in her conversations with other women, such as in her descriptions of Shug when she is ill: "She look like she ain't long for this world but dressed well for the next." She also humorously describes Albert's absences from the farm: "One good thing bout the way he never do any work round the place, us never miss him when he gone" (*CP,* 49–50). The first time Celie laughs in the novel comes after Sofia encourages Celie to take control of her life, an exchange that leads not just to laughter but also to a peace of mind Celie experiences for the first time in her marriage:

> This life soon be over, I say. Heaven last all ways.
> You ought to bash Mr. —— head open, she say. Think bout heaven later.
> Not much funny to me. That funny. I laugh. She laugh. Then us both laugh so hard us flop down on the step. . . .
> I sleeps like a baby now. (47)

Significantly, Celie's first laugh results from criticism aimed at Albert. The French feminist critic Luce Irigaray states that one of the first things women must do to assert themselves in the masculine world is to laugh among themselves. Laughter, according to Irigaray, is an indication of sexual rebellion and a means of transcending the phallic power that oppresses women.[22] Certainly this is the first time Celie has considered domestic insurrection, a rebellion that is initiated, at least partly, by the discovery of her sexuality. Her rebellious laughter is shared with another woman at the expense of the holder of phallic power in Celie's life. Around Albert, Celie's laughter is still silent at this point—which makes the act even more empowering because suppressed laughter suggests that the target, Albert, is not just an object of ridicule but also one of pity.

One of Sofia's roles in the novel is as a foil for Celie; she often acts out what Celie cannot do. Whereas Celie's meek behavior keeps her oppressed by her husband, Sofia's aggressiveness lands her in trouble as she fights the white society whose goal it is to keep her oppressed. When Sofia strikes a white man who slaps her for insubordination, she is beaten and sent to prison. Throughout this ordeal, she continues to laugh, a sign that her spirit is not broken and that her rebellion continues internally. She laughs when she talks about her husband, who tries to beat her, she laughs while working in the prison laundry, and she laughs while on parole as she teaches the

---

22. Luce Irigaray, *This Sex Which Is Not One,* trans. Catherine Porter and Carolyn Burke (Ithaca, 1985), 163.

mayor's wife to drive. Years later, when she is clerking in Celie's store and is again confronted by a white man who condescendingly calls her "auntie," Celie reports that Sofia shows the same humorous spark: "First time he try that with Sofia she ast him which colored man his mama sister marry" (*P,* 245).

The lesson Celie learns from Shug and Sofia concerns self-respect and autonomy, and the laughter she shares with them gives her the needed strength to defy her husband. Her growth culminates in a scene in which she finally verbalizes her anger at Albert and expresses feelings she had previously been able to discuss only with other women. She tells him at a dinner, in front of all her friends, that because he has mistreated her, she is leaving. He curses and threatens her, but in the company of her female friends and with her newfound strength, Celie laughs. In fact, the scene suddenly fills with the women's rebellious and unifying laughter: "Shug look at me and us giggle. Then us laugh sure nuff. Then Squeak start to laugh. Then Sofia. All us laugh and laugh." When Albert's son, Harpo, berates them and says, "It bad luck for women to laugh at men," Celie only laughs harder, commenting on bad luck: "I had enough to keep me laughing the rest of my life" (*P,* 182).

Far from being a vicious laughter solely aimed at oppressive men, this laughter expresses the women's need for autonomy, as Elsley explains: "The women are not so much laughing *at* the men as expressing in laughter their own bonding and their individual release from a system that has held them captive for so long."[23] The message in *The Color Purple* is not a misandrous screech but rather a plea for individual respect. Celie does leave Albert, but later she returns to live not as his slave but as his friend. She must leave first, however, to gain perspective and knowledge of herself, as Shug explains: "You have to git man off your eyeball, before you can see anything a'tall" (*CP,* 179). Once Celie returns, the opportunity for a sharing, equal relationship with Albert exists, as well as the potential for healing and communication. Gender differences become reversed: Celie wears pants and Albert learns to sew. Most important, Albert learns to laugh again, this time with Celie instead of Shug; he realizes Celie is "good company. . . . And he laugh" (241). In the final scenes, laughter is no longer limited to the same sex: Celie laughs with Albert, Sofia laughs with Harpo, and again Celie laughs with Shug.

In *Writing a Woman's Life,* Carolyn Heilbrun states: "In the end, the changed life for women will be marked, I feel certain, by laughter. It is the

---

23. Elsley, "Laughter as Feminine Power," in *New Perspectives,* ed. Barreca, 196.

unfailing key to a new kind of life. In films, novels, plays, stories, it is the laughter of women together that is the revealing sign, the spontaneous recognition of insight and love and freedom." Gail Griffin concurs in her description of the power of laughter among female friends: "Our enemies—whatever fools are giving us trouble, undervaluing our brilliance, insulting our magnificence—are in for it now. Our laughter is the cauldron in which they cook, until they're shriveled and bloodless. Our laughter is the explosive that blows our demons, past and present, to smithereens."[24]

Such a force is unifying, rebellious, and dangerous, enclosing and uniting those who laugh—in this case, women—in a circle of power while excluding those who oppose that laughter—men. Since this kind of laughter can reverse the hierarchy, putting women in the center and men on the margins, it is not surprising that the laughter of women is seen as culturally disruptive in novels like *The Color Purple*. Despite Walker's criticism of patriarchy, the goal is not its destruction but rather a reconstruction of a society based on mutual respect. Thadious M. Davis points out, "Walker believes in the beauty and the power of the individual, and ultimately of the group," and her "primary dream . . . is that of freedom to be one's own self." Walker herself sees her writing as a tool to make that dream a reality, and in an interview with Gloria Steinem she remarked on the soteriological power of art, that it should "make us better"; if [it] doesn't . . . then what is it for?"[25]

In Lee Smith's *Something in the Wind,* a character writes a letter telling this story:

Today I read in an anthropology book, in an obscure little footnote in an anthropology book, to be exact, about an African tribe which has a great way to test its potential chiefs. They send the young men out into the jungle and tell them to stay until they have found wisdom. It doesn't say how they find it. Anyway, after they find it, they come back and are installed as elders of the tribe. Then they go through a testing period. But if they screw up in any way while they are in this testing period—if they do anything which calls their wisdom into question—the whole tribe gathers together for a ritual feast and a

24. Carolyn Heilbrun, *Writing a Woman's Life* (New York, 1988), 129; Griffin, *Season,* 105.

25. Davis, "Alice Walker's Celebration," in *Women Writers,* ed. Prenshaw, 46; Gloria Steinem, "Do You Know This Woman? She Knows You: A Profile of Alice Walker," *MS* (June, 1982), 94.

colorful ceremony the highlight of which is they cut off the elder's head. Then the head is examined by the tribe. And if the head is laughing, they know the man was truly wise.[26]

Laughter linked to wisdom: this may explain why humor so often leads to a kind of awakening, almost epiphanic at times, for so many characters, such as Lucy Odom's realization that she cannot control others' lives, Sam Hughes's acknowledgment and acceptance of her father's death, and Celie's awareness of her own worth. Humor, then, can heal those who give as well as receive wise and witty words.

26. Lee Smith, *Something in the Wind* (New York, 1971), 19.

chapter three

CROSSING BOUNDARIES:
SCATOLOGICAL AND BLACK HUMOR

So much for moonlight and magnolias.

—RAYNA GREEN

Life does not cease to be funny when people die any more than it ceases
to be serious when people laugh.

—GEORGE BERNARD SHAW

Although traditionally there have been differences between "male" and
"female" humor—with women generally choosing as their subjects the
powerful rather than the powerless and confining their humor mainly
within female circles—recent fiction demonstrates that women writers are
closing the gender gap in some areas by exploring topics that have conven-
tionally been limited to male writers and readers, and doing so with a female perspective.

One such area is *black humor,* which could generally be characterized as
comedy about tragedy, but scholars have been unable to define the term sat-
isfactorily. More than one-fourth of the articles in Alan R. Pratt's 1993 collection, *Black Humor: Critical Essays,* attempt to define the term. Part of the
problem is distinguishing between the literary movement of the 1960s,
which includes such American authors as Joseph Heller, Kurt Vonnegut,
Ken Kesey, and Thomas Pynchon, and the literary technique, which could
be defined as humor about grotesque, macabre, or socially taboo subjects.
Both the movement and the technique rely upon the absurdity of the world
as a major premise; and both treat subjects traditionally considered tragic—
such as death, disease, war, dismemberment, and misfortune—in a humorous way. Since this study deals with post-1970 writers, our concern with
black humor in contemporary southern writing falls into the category of
literary technique.

If recent scholarship is to be believed, black humor is strictly a male
genre. Pratt's book, which is representative of the kind of work being published on black humor, includes no studies of female writers and only men-

tions a few women authors in passing. Even Flannery O'Connor, whose work provides many examples of black humor, is mentioned only as a critic of John Hawkes's work, not as a contributor to the canon. Interestingly, only one of the thirteen authors given close critical attention in Pratt's book is a southerner—Walker Percy, whose work has often been compared with O'Connor's.

The explanation for the neglect of southern female writers in the study of black humor may lie in both gender and geography. Traditionally, female humor has been less confrontational than male humor in subject and approach, whereas black humor confronts the very question of existence. Women have been expected to be more optimistic and more affirming in both life and literature, leaving the questioning of the purpose of the universe to males. Exceptions to this stereotype before 1970 can usually be explained: O'Connor's use of black humor to show the absurdity of human society applies only to characters alienated from god. Hugh Holman describes O'Connor's perspective as that of "one who has found peace and rests secure in a knowledge of herself," causing her to "look out with a kind of amused pity upon a world that is still troubled and, though it knows it not, seeking salvation from its godlessness."[1] This "amused pity" separates O'Connor from the absurdity she describes, unlike other black humorists who include themselves as players in a meaningless world, a difference that may help explain her exclusion from studies about black humor.

The general inattention to black humor in southern writing has several probable causes. Most important, although the term has only been popular since the 1960s, humor about funerals, the sick, the deformed, and death has been around for centuries, and in southern fiction, the humorists of the Old Southwest, Twain, Faulkner, and many others have all shared a penchant for such topics. In *The Burden of Southern History*, C. Vann Woodward attributes this darker focus specifically to the outcome of the Civil War rather than to a generalized pessimism about humanity so common in contemporary black humor. He claims that the Civil War taught southerners the "un-American lesson of submission" through "the experience of military defeat, occupation, and reconstruction." More recently, Fred Hobson has expanded on this theory: "The Southerner alone among Americans . . . had known defeat, and what it was not to succeed, not to prosper. The Southerner, that is, shared with the rest of the world, but not with the non-southern parts of the United States, the realization that things do not always work out. The southern writer, thus, was born with a knowledge—

1. Holman, "Detached," in *Comic Relief*, ed. S. Cohen, 99.

or soon acquired it—that the nonsouthern American writer did not have, at least in his inherited historical consciousness."[2]

What is defined as black humor in nonsouthern writing is an intrinsic part of southern literature, not a separate genre. In other words, since violence, defeat, despair, and death are common characteristics of southern writing, scholars often fail to acknowledge black humor as a separate area of study in southern literature. Because such humor appears throughout contemporary fiction by women, however, it deserves critical attention both because of what it says about southern life and because of the stereotypes it confronts.

One generalization about southern life is that southerners have violent tendencies, as Lisa Alther has noted: "Statistically the South is more violent than the rest of the United States. My brother, a sociology professor, once remarked on this fact in a speech in Alabama. A stranger phoned him that night and said it wasn't true that the South was more violent, and if he didn't get out of town he'd be sorry." Blanche McCrary Boyd also describes southerners' penchant for violence in her novel *The Revolution of Little Girls:* "Southerners are as polite as cattle, except when they're not. When they're not, they might shoot you or chase you around the yard with a hatchet." Alther also distinguishes between northern and southern aggression: "Northerners ignore you until they get to know you and then they ostracize you. Southerners bring casseroles until they get to know you and then they kill you."[3]

The humor in such violent language is dependent on the violence being metaphorical rather than literal, as in this ditty sung by Luther and Al in Lee Smith's *Oral History:*

> *Mama, don't whup Little Buford,*
> *Mama don't pound on his head,*
> *Mama don't whup little Buford,*
> *I think you should shoot him instead.*[4]

The humor here is partly due to the unexpected last line: after we are impressed by the effort of siblings to protect one another, the actual violent

2. C. Vann Woodward, *The Burden of Southern History* (Baton Rouge, 1968), 190; Hobson, *Southern Writer,* 2.

3. Lisa Alther, Introduction to *A Good Man Is Hard to Find* by Flannery O'Connor, in *Friendship,* ed. Magee, 189; Blanche McCrary Boyd, *The Revolution of Little Girls* (1991; rpr. New York, 1992), 34; Alther, quoted in Betts, Introduction to *Southern Women,* ed. Inge, 7.

4. Lee Smith, *Oral History* (1983; rpr. New York, 1984), 11–12.

intent in the last line catches us off guard. Of course, the situation would not be comic if the violence actually occurred.

Occasionally, violence is directed against objects, such as in some of the recipes in Jill McCorkle's *Ferris Beach,* which read " 'Beat the hell out of it' or 'Mash those lumps' or 'Boil that rascal till the bones fall out,' " but more often it is reflected in the communication among people who claim to love one another, especially family members. A commonplace notion about families everywhere, including the South, is that individual members vacillate between wanting to hug each other and wanting to kill each other, but what adds humor to such expressions in southern women's writing is the contrast between the violent words and the traditional image of the speaker, either a southern white female, delicate and weak, or a southern black female, nurturing and maternal.

Black humor disturbs readers for several reasons: It is not lighthearted or uplifting, and Americans generally feel guilty about laughing at the misfortunes of others as well as about mocking aspects of society that are deemed sacred, such as the family. Black humor shows little respect for such values, and for women writers, it serves as a powerful vehicle for questioning and attacking the social structures behind those values that limit or restrict the roles of women. In McCorkle's *Tending to Virginia,* the ne'er-do-well Cindy constantly bickers with her mother, and McCorkle comments: "It's a wonder Cindy doesn't die from pissed off. Her mama makes people want to die; that's all there is to it. 'Dead due to pissed off,' the doctors would say. 'Her mama did it to her.' "[5] Rather than supporting traditional expectations about parent and child, Cindy's reaction questions those roles, replacing respect with anger. Again, McCorkle's bantering between Cindy and her mother would not be humorous if Cindy did indeed die. It is the threat of death in this situation—absurd death—that creates humor.

In her novels, Tina McElroy Ansa depicts families that seem to thrive on violent intercourse. In *Baby of the Family,* the mother promises her sons she will "beat their butts till they roped like okra" if they allow any harm to come to their little sister, Lena. And although her brothers truly love Lena, when she annoys them by swinging her braids around and around her head, they admit "they were sick of her and couldn't wait until she slung her hair around one time too many and her head went flying off into a corner," a vivid and violent image that is only funny as long as it never happens.[6]

Thoughts and conversations about death, real and metaphorical, permeate other recent southern fiction. In *Ferris Beach,* Fred, the father of the

5. Jill McCorkle, *Tending to Virginia* (1987; rpr. New York, 1991), 54.
6. Tina McElroy Ansa, *Baby of the Family* (1989; rpr. San Diego, 1991), 64, 143.

family and a college math teacher, has "great ambitions of writing the perfect murder mystery, one with a plot that had to be solved mathematically" (*FB,* 2). In his quest to create the perfect theoretical murder, Fred becomes obsessed with death and begins "composing limerick obituaries for people he didn't care for" (23). He also keeps obituaries from various newspapers filed in a cigar box, "sorting them statistically by age and cause of death and geographical region" (51). While other people are attending to daily business, Fred's mind might be on scalp poisoning as a method of murder. His daughter, Kate, observes: "He kissed [his wife] again, and then at what looked like the most romantic of all moments, asked if she would call her beautician in the morning to find out a few things for his research" (140). By itself, such a request would not be humorous, but juxtaposed with a tender moment between husband and wife, readers' romantic expectations are thwarted, creating comedy.

Humor specifically dealing with death is termed *galgenhumor* (gallows humor), a word used as early as 1789 to describe jokes by prisoners about to be executed. All black humor is not gallows humor, but gallows humor is generally black. Freud called *galgenhumor* the "crudest case of humour" and gives as an example a man who asks for a scarf to wear on the way to his hanging so he will not catch cold. While this may seem callous or suggest the man is out of touch with reality, Freud claims that people laugh at such jokes because of the man's "tenacious hold upon his customary self and his disregard of what might overthrow that self and drive it to despair." In other words, whereas one might at first feel pity for the man approaching his death, instead one is distracted by the man's seeming indifference to his fate.[7]

In Alther's *Kinflicks,* the title of the first chapter, "The Art of Dying Well," prepares readers for the blackly humorous description that follows and defines a southerner's proper death, that is, one with dignity. Although it is usually considered bad taste at the dinner table to discuss such unpleasant topics as death, the family in *Kinflicks* makes a habit of it. The protagonist and narrator, Ginny, begins the novel with this description of her father: "My family has always been into death. My father, the Major, used to insist on having an ice pick next to his placemat at meals so that he could perform an emergency tracheotomy when one of us strangled on a piece of meat."[8] Although this family may not be typical and Alther's scenes are ex-

---

7. J. Jerome Zolten notes that the term *gallows* referring to jokes originally appeared in *Joe Miller's Jests* (1789), a collection of humor. "Joking in the Face of Tragedy," in *Black Humor: Critical Essays,* ed. Alan R. Pratt (New York, 1993), 306; Freud, *Jokes,* 284–85.

8. Lisa Alther, *Kinflicks* (1975; rpr. New York, 1977), 1.

aggerated for comedic effect, the significant point in the novel is the family members' fear of death not because of what comes next but because it may not occur in a dignified way.

In 1865, a relative of the nineteenth-century diarist Mary Chesnut was asked if she would prefer that all the men in her family be killed in the war, and she answered, "Yes, if their life disgraced them. There are worse things than death." In *Southern Honor*, Bertram Wyatt-Brown discusses the origins and peculiarities of such an attitude, which values death above disgrace, claiming that honor "provided a means to restrict human choices, to point a way out of chaos. Thus it helped Southern whites to make life somewhat more predictable than it would have been otherwise." Wyatt-Brown's words identify exactly the reason contemporary southern women writers choose to satirize southern honor: its purpose in maintaining the status quo. By mocking death as an honorable choice, women writers ridicule the societal structure that defines it as such. This satire is evident in the creation of characters who seem obsessed not just with dying, but with dying well. Florence King claims that "to a Southerner it is faux pas, not sins, that matter in this world," with undignified or dishonorable death being perhaps the worst social blunder of all.[9]

In one scene in Alther's novel, Ginny meets her father for coffee, and when it is brought to their table, they begin the "undeclared waiting game to see which of them would take the first sip, confirming for the other, like a canary in a coal mine, that the coffee wasn't poisoned, or the cream a host to ptomaine. It was a battle of nerves: Whose desire to drink still-warm coffee would first overcome his embarrassment at death in a public place." Significant here is the fear of dying poorly and in front of strangers. To these southerners, such exposure and humiliation are worse than simple death. Back and forth, Ginny and her father try to fool each other, pretending to sip or stalling by stirring in sugar or taking pills with water. After Ginny, distracted, takes the first sip, they both wait to see if she will collapse. A few minutes later, mistaking her anxiety about her father's heart condition for poison in the coffee, she is upset not because she expects to die at any moment but because "she was facing Eternity with safety pins holding up her bra straps," certainly in her eyes a dishonorable death, completely unacceptable to her southern sensibilities (*K,* 22–24).

Such a morbid family has not existed since Poe's Ushers, but the effect in Alther's tale is comic rather than tragic. As with the Ushers, though, obses-

---

9. Bertram Wyatt-Brown, *Southern Honor: Ethics and Behavior in the Old South* (New York, 1982), 35, 114; Florence King, *Southern Ladies and Gentlemen* (1975; rpr. New York, 1993), 12.

sion with death is inherited in Alther's fictional family. Ginny describes her mother's interest in death in seductive terms, looking for the "ultimate fuck with Death": "Mother . . . regarded Death as some kind of demon lover. The challenge, as she saw it, was to be ready for the assignation, so that you weren't distracted during consummation by unresolved earthly matters. . . . Dying *properly* was like achieving simultaneous orgasm" (*K,* 3, italics mine). Her mother, both attracted to and repulsed by death, "secretly rejoiced over each plane crash as it was reported in the papers because it meant They'd missed her again" (6). She positioned herself in planes away from the emergency exit so as not to be sucked "into the troposphere" if the exit should open in midflight, and she drove a huge black Mercedes because "it looked and drove like a hearse, Ginny suspected. Practice" (9).

Reminiscent of Twain's Emmeline Grangerford in *Huckleberry Finn,* Ginny's mother hangs morbid pictures on the wall—"handsomely framed and matted rubbings of the tombstones of [her] forebears, done in dark chalk on fine rice paper"—and she spends her free time working on her epitaph, obituary, and funeral program. In response to Ginny's childhood tantrum, during which she rages, "I *hate* you! I hope you *die!*" her mother replies, "Don't worry, I will. And so will you" (*K,* 4–5). Much like Ginny and the Major, who fear dying in a public place, Ginny's mother is more concerned about dying properly and having the funeral go smoothly than she is about the fact that she would be dead; and by focusing on absurd details, she avoids more serious questions concerning life and death.

Ginny inherits these fears, wondering who might be carrying a bomb every time she boards the "winged silver coffin" she calls a plane. She even considers carrying a bomb on the plane herself, reasoning that "the likelihood of there being *two* bomb-toting psychopaths on the same flight was so infinitesimal as to be an impossibility" (*K,* 7–8), and she spends her childhood studying photographs and hearing the macabre stories of relatives dead from every horrible disease or misfortune imaginable: "Her grandmother, Dixie Lee Hull, in a blouse with a high lace neck, who had cut her finger on a recipe card for spoon bread and had died of septicemia at age twenty-nine. Great-uncle Lester, a druggist in Sow Gap, who became addicted to cough syrup and one night threw himself under the southbound train to Chattanooga. Cousin Louella, who drove into a nest of water moccasins in an abandoned stone quarry at a family reunion in 1932. Another cousin who stuck his head out of a car window to read a historical marker about the Battle of Lookout Mountain and was sideswiped by a Mason-Dixon transport truck" (3–4). Deaths such as these easily qualify as black humor: the circumstances are absurd, the deaths are meaningless, and details such as the name of the truck that killed the cousin are insignificant yet included. These relatives did not die defending their country, their honor, or their families. They died in accidents that could easily have been avoided and that embarrass this southern family's sense of dignity.

In another of Alther's novels, *Other Women,* Marsha is described as a very smart girl who knows "everything worth knowing" except "how not to die when hit by a Bunny Bread truck in sixth grade" (*OW,* 74–75). Gallows humor is often extremely ironic, as it is here, when a truck carrying bread designed to attract children runs over one of its target customers. Later, the incident resurfaces in an ironic description of a priest who visits the Catholic school to bless the children's throats on St. Blase's Day to protect them from choking on fishbones: "The Catholics had blessings for anything that could go wrong. The priest even blessed Marsha's mother's new Amana range against grease fires and short circuits. Of course none of this helped Marsha. Though maybe the priest had simply forgotten to insure against careless Bunny Bread trucks" (119). Although Alther is also making a point about ineffectual religion, the absurdity of anyone asking for protection against an unforeseeable and bizarre event such as the Bunny Bread incident is a clear indicator of black humor.

Generally, women writers in the contemporary South have managed to find that thin line between humorous and disturbing death, a distinction not always made by male authors. John Dufresne's description of a family member's suicide in his 1994 novel *Louisiana Power & Light* is similar in content to Alther's earlier description of family death, but Dufresne's passage lacks the same hilarity: "'And then there's Aunt Elizabeth,' Fox said. 'She killed herself. . . . She ate rat poison which severely damaged her esophagus and her stomach but did not kill her. Then she threw herself down a flight of stairs. That was thought to have been an accident. . . . Then she severed an artery in her arm with a chisel.'"[10]

Both passages describe gruesome deaths, but Dufresne's description lacks the absurdity in method as well as the bizarre details. The severing of an arm with a chisel is simply disturbing; decapitation by a Mason-Dixon transport truck is ridiculous, unusual, and undignified. As with most black humor, however, a certain distance is required of the audience to find the situation humorous; it is unlikely that readers would know of anyone decapitated by a truck while reading a historical marker. By including such bizarre, concrete details in a description of death, the author helps ensure that the audience will find it comic; the chances of personal distance are much greater.

In Rita Mae Brown's *Southern Discomfort,* a bizarre death indirectly

---

10. John Dufresne, *Louisiana Power & Light* (New York, 1994), 180.

shows the importance of dignity to southerners. This is the scene in which Judge O'Brian dies at a whorehouse on "history night," dressed up like Napoleon: "Each of the girls represented a battle. By the time he got to Austerlitz he suffered a heart attack."[11] Rather than destroy his public reputation by calling for help, the prostitutes and the judge's friends change his clothes, discreetly roll his body in a rug, put it in the back of a wagon, and deposit him at his desk at the courthouse, to be found the next day by his secretary. Although all of his close friends know about his unseemly end and about the even more undignified act of rolling him in a carpet filled with mouse droppings, the fraud allows the family to maintain its public reputation and honor, and the official story protects the image of this southern gentleman.

There is more at stake here, though, than southern dignity. In "The Mode of 'Black Humor,'" Brom Weber gives this explanation: "Black humor's blackness, then, derives from its rejection of morality and other human codes ensuring earthly pattern and order, from its readiness to joke about the horror, violence, injustice, and death that rouses its indignation, from its avoidance of sentimentality by means of emotional coolness, and from its predilection for surprise and shock."[12] Judge O'Brian, who superficially represents the "pattern and order" of local society, breaks those rules by participating in the marginal society of prostitutes. Brown's humor is often ruthless in its attacks on society's hypocrites, as is apparent in this scene. By exposing hypocrisy, by surprising and shocking readers, by approaching death in such an unsentimental way, Brown calls attention to the absurdity and impracticality of a system that defines proper behavior so rigidly that it forces people to go to extremes to maintain reputable status. As Weber implies, black humor rejects traditional morality in favor of freedom of choice.

Why people find such absurd death funny rather than disturbing is a question debated endlessly. Freud suggested that we laugh at socially unacceptable ideas because breaking taboos releases a thrill within us. J. Jerome Zolten theorizes that we could just as easily cry but choose to laugh "to subvert pain." If the black humorists are right, and life is just a game without meaning, death becomes the ultimate joke played on humans. Never knowing when or how the game will end, we have few choices, and the choice made often in contemporary southern novels is to meet death at one's own time and on one's own terms, thereby subverting pain and maintaining the illusion of control over life. Suicide, tied closely with the south-

11. Rita Mae Brown, *Southern Discomfort* (1982; rpr. New York, 1988), 62–63.
12. Brom Weber, "Mode," in *Comic Imagination,* ed. Rubin, 365.

erner's sense of honor, is much more dignified than being hit by a Bunny Bread truck or being decapitated by a Mason-Dixon transport truck. The method used, the time chosen, and the order involved are all attractive to someone who has decided life has won enough rounds. Suicide is also linked to Wyatt-Brown's theory of the origins of southern honor: he argues that southerners "had a sense of oneness with ancient values—both Old Testament and classical," several times referring to the influence of ancient Rome, a society that perceived suicide as honorable death.[13]

To satirize such a philosophy, women writers create scenes in which the suicide is botched, revealing self-imposed death to be a foolish answer to life's dilemmas. If the attempts were successfully planned and executed, there would be little, if any, humor, but depending on the motivation and the method, even a successful suicide can be comic, as it is in Kaye Gibbons' *Charms for the Easy Life,* where an uncle shoots himself "after having spent two miserable years grieving over the death of Rudolph Valentino" (*EL,* 37). Even though the suicide is planned and carried out, the uncle's motive is absurd and there is adequate distance between the reader and the undeveloped character, making this suicide blackly humorous.

Like Gibbons' character, Daisy Fay's father attempts suicide in Flagg's novel for similarly absurd reasons: "Daddy says that everybody in history has a twin and that he and Mr. Harry Truman could be equals in history. Daddy and Mr. Truman both wear glasses, have a daughter, and are Democrats. I think that's why when it looked as though Thomas Dewey would win the election, Daddy jumped in the Pearl River and tried to drown himself. It took four of his friends to pull him out, one a member of the Elks Club" (*DF,* 14). Even if this attempted suicide had been successful, the scene would have been humorous because of the absurd reasons for the effort (the fallacious belief in Dewey's victory as well as the superficial connections of glasses, fatherhood, and political alignment) and the ridiculous and unneeded details in the description (the club membership of the saviors).

According to Wyatt-Brown, honor makes "the opinion of others inseparable from inner worth," and "related to brave conduct" is "family protectiveness," which explains why many fictional southerners kill themselves rather than shame the family name.[14] Through exaggeration, women's comedy reveals such thinking to be foolish. In Blanche McCrary Boyd's *The Revolution of Little Girls,* one man believes he is homosexual and kills himself to spare the family any embarrassment: "And cousin Bryce, when

---

13. Zolten, "Joking," in *Black Humor,* ed. Pratt, 306; Wyatt-Brown, *Southern Honor,* 25.
14. Wyatt-Brown, *Southern Honor,* 45, 35.

he was going to marry that girl he brought home for Christmas? Then excused himself from dinner and went upstairs and shot himself with the shotgun?" (*RLG,* 34). If this character had simply shot himself, it would not be comic, but because he waited until after dinner, thereby avoiding a social blunder, the scene is filled with black humor.

Although some characters are successful in suicide, more are content with the threat—which accomplishes a different purpose, that of venting rage against the absurdity of life without choosing to give up entirely. *Charms for the Easy Life* abounds with black humor about the "variously violent and painful means" family members have to kill themselves. Most family members threaten to drown themselves in the Pasquotank River, which flows past their door: *"If you don't stop it with that other woman, I'm going to jump in the river. If you don't stop chewing with your mouth open, I'm going to jump in the river"* (*EL,* 28). The humor in these threats comes from the juxtaposition of two such different offenses—infidelity and poor table manners—emphasizing that the threat is only that, bearing no relation to the gravity of the offense. The humor resulting from this juxtapositioning of a serious matter with something ridiculous was termed "displacement" by Freud. The focus is diverted from something serious—which would elicit pity—to something of secondary importance—which seems ludicrous, and therefore humorous, in comparison.[15]

Modern American society has generally equated suicide with moral weakness, but contemporary southern fiction sometimes connects it with personal strength instead, perhaps as a satiric link to ancient, pagan notions of honor. As Sheila Bosworth illustrates in *Slow Poison,* strong people, not weak ones, commit suicide. When a young, languid woman attempts to kill herself by jumping off a bridge, another character comments: "Drowning yourself takes some stamina. Frankly, I'm astonished the poor thing had the energy to jump into the water." In Bosworth's first novel, *Almost Innocent,* one character labels New Orleans the "suicide capital of the nation," and ironically plans to "haul out the champagne and cyanide for her farewell appearance," much as one would plan a debutante ball.[16] In this novel, as in *Slow Poison,* a woman is crazy enough to jump off the Huey P. Long Bridge but is "not crazy enough . . . to leap with her coat on," which would impede her ability to swim when she hit the water; instead, she leaves the coat folded carefully on the car seat, revealing to all that she never intended to die, only to protest (*AI,* 14).

---

15. Freud, *Jokes,* 289.

16. Sheila Bosworth, *Slow Poison* (1992; rpr. Baton Rouge, 1998), 52; Sheila Bosworth, *Almost Innocent* (1984; rpr. Baton Rouge, 1996), 104–105.

Southern fiction provides many examples of failed suicide that are blackly humorous and ironic because the characters have decided that life is absurd and not worth living but are unable to assert enough control over fate even to end that life. It is as if life plays a triple trick on the suicide-survivors: life is meaningless, death is unavailable as an alternative, and, often, no one has even noticed the attempt to die. Lisa Alther's novels keenly illustrate this turn of fate. In *Other Women,* a therapist and her patient both have failed suicides in their pasts. Caroline recounts the time she was depressed over the pettiness of her life: "I turned on the gas oven and stuck my head in. It was so dirty I decided to clean it first. By the time I finished, the boys were awake from their naps." After hearing this, her therapist, Hannah, remembers her own attempt: "A couple of months after the children died, she walked off across the frozen lake, leaving Arthur a good-bye note. After a couple of hours shivering beside a snow drift, when he hadn't arrived to talk her out of it, she trudged home," only to find her husband had not even noticed she was missing (*OW,* 203–204). Both women are diverted from completing the planned suicide by the trivial things in life—a dirty oven, cold weather—and the point is clear: it is for the trivial things that they live. A failed suicide attempt teaches this, but a successful one does not, as Hannah realizes and expresses later in the novel, when one of her patients, Mary Beth, does manage to kill herself by slashing her wrists: "Farewell, Mary Beth, thought Hannah. May you finally find some peace. Though she suspected suicide wasn't a long-term solution. Mary Beth would probably have to come back as a barber, until she learned the proper use for razors" (335).

In *Kinflicks,* Ginny decides to end her life after both her parents die and she finds she has "no place to go and no one to love and her underwear needed washing." Coming from this family so obsessed with death, it would seem to be easy enough for Ginny to end her life, but the novel's final scene is so full of black humor that it quickly evolves into slapstick. Ginny tries to drown herself several times, but the rope attached to the rock designed to drag her under is too long. Becoming discouraged with that method, she takes a rifle and bullets to a cave where no one will find her, only to find that the bullets do not fit her gun. On her third try, she makes a small, experimental cut on her wrist with a knife, but much like Hannah and Caroline, she becomes distracted by a trivial thing: watching the process of coagulation. Eventually, believing she has failed in death as she has failed in life, she decides she must live: "Like most of her undertakings, her proposed suicide had degenerated into burlesque. Apparently she was condemned to survival" (*K,* 516–18). Harking back to Dorothy Parker's blackly humorous poem, "Resumé," Ginny decides that the methods she might use to kill herself are so horrible and ineffective, she "might as well live."

Condemned to life or condemned to death, writers use black humor to laugh at fate, perhaps as a protest against the absurdity of both survival and demise. Rita Mae Brown's *Venus Envy* is based on such a premise: The protagonist, Frazier Armstrong, is told by her doctor that she is dying of lung cancer and that she should put her life and relationships in order. This she does by writing letters to her family and friends, telling them what faults and virtues she sees in each of them, and revealing that she is a lesbian. Ironically, soon after mailing the letters, she learns that she is not dying. The rest of the novel concerns Frazier's rewards and punishments for being honest.

Frazier's attempt at optimism in the face of tragedy is honorable. She notes, "Dying's not so bad. At least I won't have to answer the telephone," and when she looks at the prim, sentimental wallpaper with bouquets of flowers, she decides, in words reminiscent of Oscar Wilde's famous line, "one of us has to go."[17] Fortunately, Frazier has a sense of humor about life and death, which helps her survive her honesty. There is even a joke in the novel about two frightening and incurable diseases: "Listen to this. A guy goes to the doctor with his wife. She's been feeling bad for a while so they run a battery of tests on her and she's maybe forty, you know, not too old. Two weeks later the doctor calls the guy in his office and says, 'We've reviewed the results of all these tests, Mack, but we can't quite pinpoint your wife's disease. I know this sounds crazy but she's either got Alzheimer's or AIDS.' Alzheimer's or AIDS? The guy can't believe it. 'What do I do?' he says. The doctor says, 'Take her for a nice long walk in the forest and then leave her there. If she finds her way home, don't fuck her'" (*VE,* 86). Such humor in the face of death is a reminder that laughter is close to tears. It also marks Brown's humor as distinctly female, pointing out the inevitability and absurdity of death but then looking for the upbeat side of the worst situation, affirming the life that is left by laughing.

This attitude is usually not shared by characters created by male writers, who more often see life as futile and meaningless, suggesting a question about southern female writers' inclusion in the genre of black humor. If black humorists believe in life's futility and absurdity, how can Brown's or Alther's or Gibbons' novels, which ultimately have optimistic themes, be considered examples of black humor? Some critics would say they are not. Thomas Kuhlman, for instance, notes that "true gallows humor has no moral overtones, is not preachy, is not reverent. It has no purpose other than

17. Rita Mae Brown, *Venus Envy* (New York, 1993), 1.

its participants' psychological well-being."[18] This is an important difference in fiction written by women, in which gallows humor may have an important moral overtone, however subtle.

The most obvious instance of black humor in Fannie Flagg's *Fried Green Tomatoes at the Whistle Stop Café* is tied specifically to a feminist message about domestic violence. The most shocking and yet comic incident in this novel is the murder of Frank Bennett. Bennett—who beats his wife, Ruth, until she leaves him and then follows her to take back his child and physically abuse Ruth again—is killed in self-defense by Ruth's protectors, who are society's underlings: women and blacks. To cover up the death, Bennett's car is sunk, his head is buried along with hogs' carcasses, and his body is boiled with the pork to be used in the barbecue sold at the café.

This is a grisly scene, and Flagg describes it aptly: "Later that afternoon, when Grady and the two detectives from Georgia were questioning his daddy about the missing white man, Artis had nearly fainted when one of them came over and looked right in the pot. He was sure the man had seen Frank Bennett's arm bobbing up and down among the boiling hogs. But evidently, he hadn't, because two days later, the fat Georgia man told Big George that it was the best barbecue he had ever eaten, and asked him what his secret was."[19] As this example shows, women's humor often attacks authority figures, in this case the entire patriarchal structure that protects people like Frank Bennett, allowing those whom he abuses to take control of their lives and protect themselves. The murder and ensuing cannibalism somehow seem justified, and one cannot help but smile at the double meaning in George's answer to the detective's question: "the secret's in the sauce."

Although other southern fiction by women containing black humor may not send as strong a message as Flagg's novel, one thing that becomes clear throughout the canon is that there are worse things than death to southerners: dishonor, disgrace, defeat. Southern black humor reminds readers of their vulnerability and the inevitability of death. Faced with the choice of how to react to this fate, southern women have chosen to laugh, not with traditional black humorists' sense of futility but with the knowledge that neither laughter nor tears will change the outcome.

The mother of Ginny Babcock in *Kinflicks* tells her daughter when she has her first period that "what was happening was indeed horrible—but quite

---

18. Thomas Kuhlman, "Gallows Humor for Scaffold Settings: The Role of Humor in High Stress Service," *WHIMSY,* IV (1988), 129.

19. Fannie Flagg, *Fried Green Tomatoes at the Whistle Stop Café* (1987; rpr. New York, 1988), 367.

normal. That bleeding like a stuck pig every month was the price exacted for being allowed to scrub some man's toilet bowl every week" (*K*, 32). This type of humor can be termed *scatological,* yet another area that has traditionally been considered male. Although originally scatology was a branch of science that used the feces in diagnoses, literary scholars have expanded the definition to include a preoccupation with or a study of obscenity. Obscenities in this sense include not only bodily excretions and functions but also sexual organs and obscene language, especially when written about in a graphic, earthy tone. (The somewhat subtle difference between sexual humor and scatological humor, by this definition, is that the former deals with the sexual act whereas the latter deals with the physical organs and secretions.)

Scatological humor, of course, is not limited to southern literature, but the South does have a relatively long history of such comedy. Bawdy humor in America can be traced back to the humorists of the Old Southwest and to the frontier explorers who were so imaginative and graphic in their storytelling and, before that, to the seventeenth- and eighteenth-century European satirists, who considered human bodily functions a viable topic for humor. Cohen and Dillingham characterize such humor as filled with "stark, realistic details and off-color, bawdy comments." It is often "earthy [and] shocking to the gentle reader," which is one reason Cohen and Dillingham categorize it as "masculine humor."[20] And while this may have been more true before the twentieth century, this "masculine" label no longer accurately describes southern scatological humor.

In the twentieth century, the tradition of scatological humor by males in the South can be traced from Faulkner to John Kennedy Toole and beyond, but early in the century, only a few brave female writers attempted this type of humor. Carson McCullers is one who did, and she includes several scatological situations in her short novel *The Ballad of the Sad Café*. McCullers writes that Miss Amelia's feud with a relative is so antagonistic that "when they chanced to pass each other they spat on the side of the road," and later Miss Amelia reveals that she keeps her extracted kidney stones in a velvet box, eventually having them "set as ornaments in a watch chain."[21] Significantly, Miss Amelia is a "masculine" character whose actions are not in sync with those of the other female characters of her town.

In *To Kill a Mockingbird,* Harper Lee gives a subtle scatological description of Mr. Avery through the eyes of a young girl, Scout Finch: "At first we saw nothing but a kudzu-covered front porch, but a closer inspection

---

20. Cohen and Dillingham, *Humor,* xv, xi.

21. Carson McCullers, *"The Ballad of the Sad Café" and Other Stories* (1951; rpr. New York, 1991), 7, 35–36.

revealed an arc of water descending from the leaves and splashing in the yellow circle of the street light, some ten feet from source to earth, it seemed to us. Jem said Mr. Avery misfigured, Dill said he must drink a gallon a day, and the ensuing contest to determine relative distances and respective prowess only made me feel left out again, as I was untalented in this area."[22] Like Miss Amelia, tomboy Scout is a masculine character, and her comment about feeling "left out again" is significant, not just because she lacks the physiological tool to participate in this contest, but also because women have generally been excluded from the realm of scatological humor, discouraged from hearing, making, or laughing at such jokes. McCullers' and Lee's scenes also exemplify the subtlety of early female scatological humor. Spitting and urinating are relatively mild acts, and the descriptions are exceptionally vague and lacking in detail.

In her study of gender differences in humor, Regina Barreca quotes psychologist Rose Laub Coser: "If you were a boy, having a sense of humor meant pouring salt on the head of the girl who sat in front of you. . . . If you were a girl, having a sense of humor meant laughing when someone poured salt on your head." This example shows, first, that girls are taught to laugh at their own misfortunes and embarrassments rather than at others' —part of the "humane humor rule"—especially southern ladies, whose traditions emphasize dignity and deportment, and second, that males stereotypically enjoy physical humor—slapstick, literal, scatological humor— more than females do. But Barreca also points out that in situations that involve only women, women can be very funny indeed, with few limitations on the topics discussed. Other women scholars have concurred, among them Anne Jones: "We could say the body has been the lifeblood of Southern humor. The racial body, the female body, the grotesque body, all have been offered up to the god of Southern laughter. Southern women love body jokes of all kinds."[23] The difference is that in the past, women's delight in bawdy and body humor was confined to the kitchen—or to "tomboys" like Miss Amelia and Scout—and it is only recently that women have felt enfranchised enough to explore, to participate in, and to share their scatological observations. Judging from the number, variety, and explicitness of examples found in fiction, gender plays little part in the creation of scatological jokes today.

In *The Last Laugh: Form and Affirmation in the Contemporary American Comic Novel,* Ronald Wallace claims there are two main purposes for the inclusion of scatological humor: first, to remind people of their "animal

---

22. Harper Lee, *To Kill a Mockingbird* (1960; rpr. New York, 1962), 55.
23. Barreca, *They Used to Call Me Snow White,* 7; Jones, "Incredible," 417.

nature," and second, to "comment on the modern obsession with cleanliness."[24] Although this may be true, there are other reasons writers use scatological humor, especially southern women writers, the first being a declaration of equality. Men have been allowed, even encouraged, to make their sexual organs and bodily functions a subject for comedy, but until recently, women have been discouraged from considering the female body a viable topic for discussion and satire, at least in mixed company. Passed off for centuries by men as unexplainable lunacy, such subjects as the female hormonal cycle, menstruation, and menopause are finally being explored with honesty and humor by women writers—who often aim the humor at the cultural power in their lives: men.

Rayna Green explains that women—in private—have always made jokes at the expense of men in order to "vent their anger at males."[25] Flagg's *Fried Green Tomatoes* has numerous scatological episodes that do just that; in one chapter, Flagg has enormous fun with the male obsession with "having balls." In a highly ironic monologue, Evelyn decides having balls is "the most important thing in this world" and that she must have some of her own if she is to be taken seriously: "If Ed loved her so much, why couldn't he give her one of his? A ball transplant . . . That's right. Or, maybe she could get two from an anonymous donor. That's it, she'd buy some off a dead man and she could put them in a box and take them to important meetings and bang them on the table to get her way. Maybe she'd buy four." Flagg extends the humor of the double meaning in the title to the following chapter, which is taken from a newspaper headline announcing fundraising for the physical education department of the high school—"Benefit for New Balls"—questioning why a woman should have to be physiologically like a man to get respect and recognition (*FGT,* 276–78).

Public jokes by women demeaning the sexual organs of men have certainly been rare and somewhat taboo in American literature until recently, as have jokes about women's sexual experimentations. In Flagg's novel, Evelyn joins the Women's Community Center and attends group sessions, but her inhibitions eventually overcome her adventurous spirit: "She had wanted to belong, but when the woman suggested that next week they bring a mirror so they could all study their vaginas, she never went back" (*FGT,* 43). Contrasted with the chapter about the male obsession with testicles, this excerpt illustrates the unequal and absurd limitations American patriarchal culture puts on women—which women accept by adhering to

24. Wallace, *The Last Laugh,* 20.
25. Rayna Green, "Magnolias Grow in Dirt: The Bawdy Lore of Southern Women," in *Speaking for Ourselves,* ed. Alexander, 27.

such boundaries: Men are allowed to talk about, boast about, and discuss their sexual organs, whereas women are afraid even to look at theirs.

But in *Confessions of a Failed Southern Lady,* Florence King exaggerates the role sexual organs play in the lives of her female relatives, perhaps as shock therapy—just as Flannery O'Connor used violence in her stories for the "hard of hearing" and "almost blind." One character, Evelyn, is convinced that she is not crazy but only has "female troubles." Afraid her womb is going to fall out in public, she carries around an empty pickle jar. In one scene, in the middle of a crowd, she "yells 'Here it comes!' and squats down over the jar, awaiting its arrival" (*FSL,* 56). Although King's stories are highly exaggerated for satire's sake, generally one of the advantages in reading women's literature is that readers finally get an accurate description of how real women act, especially when they are alone or only with other women, something that male writers can only imagine. The "real" woman is often a surprise to men but usually a relief to other women; women can finally laugh at themselves, realizing that they are not alone in their problems or dilemmas.

Hormones and their role in women's lives is another topic discussed and satirized, as in Lisa Alther's *Bedrock,* in which Clea claims that hormones have "always been her recreational drug of choice."[26] Rather than ignoring or downplaying such an important aspect of the female psyche, in Flagg's novel Evelyn struggles with the changes menopause has made in her personality: "That menopause has hit her with a vengeance! She said, not only does she want to hit Ed in the head, but lately, she's having fantasies in her mind where she dresses up in black clothes and goes out at night and kills all the bad people with a machine gun" (*FGT,* 255). By laughing at impulses like Evelyn's, women can use humor to create a sexual unity among themselves, first by recognizing that such feelings exist and are as valid as male sexual sensibilities.

In *Tending to Virginia,* Jill McCorkle includes a scene that causes fear and recognition in every woman, either from actual experience or from dread of encountering such a problem:

> "I can't find it," Cindy had wailed and run to the door of the kitchen where Virginia and Madge were sitting at the table. She had stood there, a jar of Vaseline in one hand, the other hand held way out to the side and her underwear around her knees.
>
> "What are you talking about?" Madge asked. "You put your pants on before your daddy comes in here."

---

26. Lisa Alther, *Bedrock* (1990; rpr. New York, 1991), 3.

"What am I gonna do?" Cindy pulled up her underwear and squatted down in the doorway.

"Cindy Sinclair, what on earth is wrong with you?" Madge asked and Virginia had to turn her head to the side to keep from laughing though it didn't work.

"It's not funny, Ginny!" Cindy's face was fire-red and tears were welling up in her eyes. "I've got a tampon up me and I can't find it!" (166)

This scene is revealing in terms of both gender and generation. Men would not likely find this scene humorous, yet women have always been expected to laugh at exclusively male humor, pretending to understand and relate to something that is alien to their experience. For example, in those "hit in the testicles" scenes so overused in films, a man laughs in recognition, whereas a woman feels pressured to laugh in sympathy. Why, then, would men not feel the same pressure to empathize over a lost-tampon scene?

The older woman in the scene, Madge, believes not only that such topics are unmentionable—let alone unfunny—but also that tampons should not even be used by "nice" women. She comments: "Hush. I never heard of such in my life," and "I told you not to wear those things, it's not natural to wear those things. It's just not right what you girls do, swimming and carrying on during that time" (*TV,* 167). Her reaction to Cindy's tampon crisis illustrates that the widespread use and appreciation of scatological humor is relatively new for women, and that older women tend to find scatological subjects crude and unladylike.

This generational limitation, especially tied to social class, is supported in many novels. Evelyn in *Fried Green Tomatoes* stops examining her breasts "because one time she had felt a lump and almost fainted." This incident alone is mildly comic, but the author goes on to show the absurdity of such denial: "Fortunately, it turned out to be Kleenex that had stuck to her bra in the wash" (*FGT,* 61). Sheila Bosworth's character Tipping, in *Slow Poison,* feels the same need to deny the existence of her body, in this case as a way of denying her own mortality. To admit to having a body is to admit to the inevitable dissolution of that body: "She continually visualized her insides as a lethal mess, seething with disease. Every time she lowered her underpants to sit on the toilet, she was careful not to look down in case there was any blood on them. Not the menstrual blood that had stopped coming; the blood Tipping pictured on her underpants now was one of the Seven Hundred Signs of Approaching Death. She feared that Death had established squatter's rights on her internal organs and was foraging through to her outerlayers like Sherman through Georgia to the sea. . . . Tipping without exception had vomited and urinated and defecated and flushed the toilet with her eyes closed since she was thirty-five" (*SP,* 32). The absurdity of these older characters' actions is that they have not given up responsibility for their bodies; they have given up only an acknowledgment of them, an attitude clearly tied both to social class and to age.

Younger characters of any class tend toward the literal and the scatological. In describing southern humor and its tendency toward the concrete, George Koon states that the "agrarian economy probably explains this literal approach best. Life close to the land just does not call for much abstraction," and even though much of the new southern literature is set in cities, the remnants of rural life still remain in the language of the southerner, especially in its scatological references. In Kaye Gibbons' *A Virtuous Woman,* Jack remarks, "Burr's daddy . . . always treated me like I didn't have enough sense to pour piss out of a boot with the instructions on the heel."[27] Barbara Kingsolver uses the metaphor "life had delivered Sandi a truckload of manure with no return address" (*BT,* 66). These types of phrases are more than word play; they characterize southerners, and especially southern writers, as clearly in touch with their agrarian roots, no matter how long they have been living in Atlanta or Baton Rouge or Chapel Hill.

Rita Mae Brown, whose works are full of scatological episodes, describes a certain perfume as smelling "like cat's pee" (*SD,* 5), compares a town's conservative predilection to "blocked bowels,"[28] and comments, "My mother says women *are* like flies. They'll settle on shit or on sugar" (*VE,* 23). Coming from a male writer, these phrases would be unremarkable, but coming from a female author, they are practically revolutionary. Doris Betts suggests that scatological humor is a part of Brown's personal sense of humor. When Betts described her work with Brown on the Literary Committee of the National Endowment, she commented that Brown's "ability to shout 'Batshit' at moments I might have gotten hung up on Roberts Rules of Order was refreshing."[29] Brown's word choice reflects her freedom to use humor to disrupt society's system, thereby challenging traditional order, and it is a reminder that chaos may not always be a negative state.

With occasional exceptions, however, most of the scatological activity in novels is still limited to characters who are rural, children, animals, or men—and these characters often receive criticism from older women for

27.   George Koon, ed., *A Collection of Classic Southern Humor: Fiction and Occasional Fact by Some of the South's Best Storytellers,* (Atlanta, 1984), I, ix; Kaye Gibbons, *A Virtuous Woman* (1989; rpr. New York, 1990), 80–81.

28.   Rita Mae Brown, *Six of One* (1978; rpr. New York, 1988), 68.

29.   Doris Betts to the author, December, 1993.

their behavior. In *Ugly Ways,* the culprit is a friend of husband Ernest. Once, in a drunken stupor, the friend had turned "the wrong way, had wandered into the living room mistaking it for the bathroom, unzipped his pants, and peed on one of the low side tables next to the sofa." Ernest's wife, showing her disapproval and her age, never lets Ernest forget the episode, continually shaming him: "Any time Ernest dared to mention a friend or coworker in Mudear's hearing, she would say, 'I hope he ain't gonna come into my house and pee on the floor'" (*UW,* 49–50). In *Daisy Fay and the Miracle Man,* Daisy Fay's father is criticized for a similar episode by his Aunt Helen because "he put her boyfriend's picture on the back of the toilet seat once" (26).

It also seems more acceptable for female children, rather than grown women, to be involved in scatological episodes, perhaps because little girls have not yet been indoctrinated with social rules and customs. In *Rubyfruit Jungle,* Molly Bolt mixes raisins with rabbit droppings to punish a boastful playmate (16), and in *Ellen Foster,* Ellen is bored during rest time at school, and so delights in the body-as-toy: "I cannot sleep in that position so I fake it. There is nothing to do but fill up your pencil tray with spit" (*EF,* 53). And finally, in Flagg's novel, eleven-year-old Daisy Fay describes her own scatological problems: "Daddy hated being a soldier and was busted six times. Whenever he got a furlough, he wouldn't go back until the MPs came for him. One time when I was in the bathroom, they were banging on the door hollering for Daddy. Momma wanted me to hurry up and finish so I could say good-bye, but all that knocking made me nervous and Momma believes that is the reason I have to have so many enemas now. Momma blames the Military Police for ruining what had been a very successful toilet training period" (*DF,* 17).

This new freedom for women writers is generally refreshing, opening the door to explore the scatological and its uses in literature, such as in development of theme. By utilizing the longstanding negative associations with scatological functions, a writer can say a great deal with a simple act. The symbol can be a very common one, such as is found in the comparison Idgie uses in *Fried Green Tomatoes:* "I swear, I don't know what people are using for brains anymore. Imagine those boys: They're terrified to sit next to a nigger and have a meal, but they'll eat eggs that came right out of a chicken's ass" (55). In this one line, the issue of racial prejudice is summed up as ludicrous. The unjust and irrational thinking behind racist behavior is clarified by reducing everyone to the same animal level and reminding readers that no one is superior.

In her second novel, *She Flew the Coop,* Michael Lee West explores the relationships among the themes in her subtitle—*A Novel Concerning Life,*

Death, Sex and Recipes in Limoges, Louisiana—often scatologically. At times, the novel scathingly satirizes sex and religious practice, often showing both to be selfish acts tied closely to primitive and scatological animal instincts. In one scene, the lascivious Reverend Kirby seduces sixteen-year-old Olive Nepper in the belfry of the First Baptist Church. While they have sex, pigeons fly in circles above his back, splattering his sweater with "white commas . . . against the red wool." In addition to being a fitting symbol of heaven's opinion of this man's despicable behavior, Olive notes a second symbol in the birds' actions, comparing the minister's act of "love" to a bird's act of elimination: "She had to admit, the whole thing had weird symmetry. While the reverend deposited one thing, the pigeons deposited something else. Except for the birds, everybody got a souvenir" (*SF,* 8–9). In this simple comparison, the reverend's actions are aptly described as no more meaningful than the birds' defecation.

A similar cynical opinion about sex is expressed at various times by other characters in the novel. Henry, an adulterous husband who has been caught by his wife, explains to her, "Hell, that woman didn't mean anything to me. Being with her wasn't any different from peeing into a urinal" (*SF,* 303). At another time, Henry's mistress comments, "I fell in love, hard. When it hits you, it's like peeing all over yourself. You just can't hold it in," suggesting an ambiguous opinion of physical love (120). On the one hand, sex is an overwhelming and all-consuming need that evidences itself whether people want it to or not, and it is a temporarily pleasant release of pent-up feelings; but on the other hand, it can be slightly disagreeable once the experience is over and is impossible to take back.

Throughout the novel, West makes humorous, scatological references to religion as a comment on the often mundane rather than ethereal inspiration behind religious fervor. In one scene, Reverend Kirby's "forehead wrinkled the way it always did when a sermon was coming on. (He felt the same way with bowel movements; sometimes it was hard to tell the difference.)" It is not just insincere ministers, however, who confuse bodily functions and spiritual meaning. As they grow older, contemplating death and heaven, Methodists, "become obsessed with bowel movements," perhaps, like Reverend Kirby, mistaking physical patience and reward for the spiritual (*SF,* 173).

Perhaps the strangest symbolic scatology is found in Gail Godwin's *The Odd Woman.* The novel is partly concerned with the life of Jane Clifford, an unmarried professor, and her attempts to break free from a destructive relationship with a married man. One of the subplots, however, deals with a bizarre criminal known as the Enema Bandit: "For nearly two years, this person had prowled the softly lit streets near campus, a stocking pulled over his face, carrying his pistol and his enema bag. His victims were always women. He abided by a certain self-imposed decorum. He never broke into a dwelling. . . . He had been known on two occasions to desist gallantly. Once when an older woman, who had just lost her husband, broke down and cried, and told him of her sorrow; and once when a young girl, whose roommate was getting the enema, begged him not to because she had her period"(*TOW,* 28). Strangely, this odd new form of rape is described by Jane as a "treatment" and a "remedy." In effect, the bandit is doing to women what, symbolically, they need to do to themselves: get rid of the "shit" in their lives, in this case, a man who is detrimental to Jane's growing awareness and autonomy. Although ostensibly Jane gets rid of the "shit" by leaving her lover in New York City, at home she finds herself alone and missing him. She still waits in anticipation for his phone call asking her forgiveness and begging her to take him back. As the novel ends, she is lying in bed, and she hears *"someone . . . sliding down the low roof of her duplex, just outside the bedroom window, trying to keep his foothold in soft-soled shoes,"* and she believes it is the enema bandit at last, ready to administer the remedy that will, theoretically, cure her finally and completely of her dependence on her married lover (418).

Because of its reputation as a low form of humor, some people might see the emergence of scatological humor in fiction by women as a devolution, but the recognition and incorporation of scatological humor is a kind of liberation. Like the use of black humor, the use of scatological humor is one more barrier broken, one more limitation challenged, and one less secret kept, allowing women to explore areas once considered taboo.

chapter four

UNBUCKLING THE BIBLE BELT:
RELIGIOUS AND SEXUAL SATIRE

If we couldn't laugh, we would all go insane.

—JIMMY BUFFETT

It's hard to be funny when you have to be clean.

—MAE WEST

One of the strengths of humor, specifically satire, is that it can usually speak truth without alienating listeners, especially when the topic of discussion is considered sacred. Satire, of course, is nothing new to southern literature; the South of the seventeenth and eighteenth centuries was populated with satirists, and the nineteenth century produced perhaps the greatest American satirist of all: Mark Twain. What is new in the South, however, is the prevalence, audacity, and target of women's satire. By giving voice to a topic not often discussed publicly, women admit its significance, and by laughing about it openly, women exert control over its influence in their lives, limiting the guilt that Lillian Smith identifies as the "biggest crop raised in Dixie."[1]

Southern writers seem keenly aware of the problems and paradoxes of the region, often using fiction as a means of questioning and exploring those conflicts. This is especially true of women's satire, which tends to attack the patriarchal system women live in but have had little part in structuring and administering. Satire in novels produced by southern women has become very common, more so since the 1970s, when women writers began to articulate their criticisms of the South and its treatment and depiction of women. In *The Folk of Southern Fiction,* Merrill Skaggs states: "Literature was the last battleground on which the values of the Old South were tested; as critics have observed repeatedly, in literature the South won an unconditional victory."[2] With the writings of the contemporary South

---

1. Lillian Smith, *Killers of the Dream* (1949; rpr. New York, 1994), 103.
2. Merrill Maguire Skaggs, *The Folk of Southern Fiction* (Athens, Ga., 1972), 4.

in mind, it is necessary to qualify Skaggs's statement: Literature has tested the values of the male South, but the battle still continues for women.

In contemporary satire by women, cultural and social customs are often made to appear pretentious and absurd through exaggeration, calling into question all that the traditional male southerner, whose voice was more often recorded and heard, has proclaimed sacred and true. Two such subjects are religion and sex. Linking them may seem odd, but they are closely related in southern life and fiction. Writers often tie religion to sex in their works, perhaps because traditionally southerners have seen them both as inherent needs, both yielding passion and both producing guilt. Lee Smith has commented on the interrelationship of the two in her early life: "So religion and sex—you know, excitement, passion—were all together. I couldn't differentiate between sexual passion and religious passion. This was what we all did on dates, was go to the revival. It was a turn-on."[3] In addition, religion and sexual relationships have traditionally been dominated by men. By targeting those men, women expose their weaknesses and biases, placing themselves in the position of power instead.

Religion and the South had been linked long before H. L. Mencken popularized the term *Bible Belt* as a designation of the region. In dissecting religion and questioning the validity of its role in contemporary life, authors often experience a fierce conflict between their long-held beliefs and their artistic vision, using humor as a means of exploring that tension, as Susan Ketchin explains in *The Christ-Haunted Landscape: Faith and Doubt in Southern Fiction:* "For some the tension is dealt with in part through humorous, ironic detachment and satire. Such irony is the result of these authors' caring deeply about the traditions that nurtured them and of their commitment to the truths that seem to be in direct conflict with those traditions."[4]

As Ketchin's title and this quotation suggest, women writers grapple with faith and doubt, exploring to what degree traditional, patriarchal religion should play a part in their lives. Of course, contemporary male writers also satirize religion (and sex); two novels that incorporate both are Harry Crews's *A Feast of Snakes,* rife with religious fanatics and desperate characters searching for love and faith but settling for much less, and Howard Owen's *Fat Lightning,* an extremely dark look at religious fanaticism and the impossibility of maintaining love in modern life. The main difference between male and female religious satire generally comes down to gender

3. Susan Ketchin, *The Christ-Haunted Landscape: Faith and Doubt in Southern Fiction* (Jackson, Miss., 1994), 45–46.

4. *Ibid.,* xviii.

perspective and satirical target. Whereas male writers may attack the institutions of church and marriage, female writers attack not only the institutions but also the male figures behind those institutions, who have traditionally dictated policy and behavior for women throughout the centuries, marking women as representatives of Eve, forever tempting men away from God with the apple of sex. In short, although men may view religion as absurd or meaningless, women may also see it as oppressive and destructive.

There may be no better example of the synthesis of institution and man than the minister or preacher, a common target of female satire. Rayna Green explains that preachers "take the brunt of many jokes, and one can understand, given the Southern church's rigorous control over women's lives, why parson stories are true favorites."[5] Far from being honorable men of God, fictional men of the cloth are flawed individuals who warrant laughs more than respect. Rather than being called by God, they more often receive noninspired callings to preach, such as Bobbie Ann Mason's Thomas Wilburn in *Feather Crowns,* who hears God speaking to him out of the sky, never realizing the voice comes from "one of his sons . . . hiding in a tree," or Vicki Covington's Cal Gaines in *Gathering Home,* who grows up going to baseball games with his sportscaster father, hiding in the dirt under the bleachers. His friend suggests this experience might be the reason why he became a preacher: "Staring up at people's asses all the time. You know, it must have given you a certain view of life, like there was work to do in the world, a bad side to people."[6] By denying preachers divine callings, women writers strip them of their authority to dictate the lives of those who trust them, exposing them as mere con men rather than mediators between God and humans.

In fiction, ministers are often irreverent men who use their position for personal gain and try to justify their actions in the name of God, like the preacher in West's *She Flew the Coop,* who disappears from Shreveport, Louisiana. When authorities find him "a month later in Hawaii, preaching on Waikiki Beach, offering to translate for those who spoke in tongues," they ask him why he would do this, and he answers, "Well, that's simple. I got a phone call from God. . . . I couldn't make out but one word. . . . Honolulu" (*SF,* 118).

Father O'Donnell, in Ansa's *Baby of the Family,* always shows up "magically" at the window whenever a woman in the McPherson household "walked around the house in her bra and panties." Once he enters the

5. Green, "Magnolias," in *Speaking,* ed. Alexander, 24.

6. Bobbie Ann Mason, *Feather Crowns* (New York, 1993), 66; Vicki Covington, *Gathering Home* (1988; rpr. New York, 1990), 143.

house, he starts up the stairs saying in a voice reminiscent of fairy-tale wolves: "Oh, good woman, good woman, open the door, open the door. It's only I, your parish priest, come to visit your lovely family, lovely family," to which the grandmother replies with one of those violent southern answers: "That damn fool was gonna come right on up here. I don't care if he is a priest, somebody is gonna shoot him dead one day. . . . I can see the headline now: 'Irate Mate Shoots Intruding Paddy Priest'" (*BF,* 65–66). Examples like this help explain women's anger at male religious leaders. James Cobb claims this anger stems from "their suspicion that ministers pursued their calling out of the desire to avoid manual labor while enjoying easy access to the good food and sexual favors provided by the female faithful," a motivation that would anger both men and women but perhaps for different reasons: men because of the laziness and women because of the lechery.[7]

By "humanizing" preachers, women writers reduce their power, often making them look absurd. In Godwin's *A Southern Family,* Father Zachary has a flat tire on the way to a cemetery service and so "simply pulled off to the side of the highway and stood there with his thumb out, his long black skirts whipping around the bottom of his coat in the January winds, until one of the mourners' cars picked him up."[8] With any other character, this scene would not be particularly comic—except, perhaps, for the black humor found in anyone having to hitchhike to a funeral—but because the character is a preacher, the scene is oddly funny; it puts what society has determined as sacred and spiritual on the mundane level, where the rest of the world resides. And by association, the patriarchal power of the preacher is questioned because of his inability to save himself. Satirically portraying religious leaders as more like humans and less like God, these writers remind readers that no one belongs on a pedestal.

Significantly, contemporary authors generally do not attack religion, but rather the people who take advantage of others in the name of God. Televangelists, especially, are targets of sharp criticism, as well they might be, considering the scandals that have filled the newspapers in recent years, with the satire becoming much less tolerant and much more bitter. The novels of Fannie Flagg are especially critical of religious predators. Reminiscent of the King and Duke in *Huckleberry Finn,* who are only out for profit, her religious con men rely on the gullibility of common folk. Billy Bundy, Flagg's radio preacher in *Daisy Fay and the Miracle Man,* sells "auto-

7. James C. Cobb, " 'Damn Brother, I Don't Believe I'd a-Told That!' Humor and the Cultural Identity of the American South,' " *Southern Cultures,* I (1995), 484.

8. Gail Godwin, *A Southern Family* (New York, 1987), 89.

graphed pictures of the Last Supper" (*DF,* 53) and counts his money in the back room of the Bon Ton Café because it is the "only place he can get alcohol after church" (61). Together with Daisy Fay's father—who tells his daughter that "the Epistles were the wives of the Apostles" (28)—Billy concocts an elaborate scheme to make money: Daisy Fay will be lost at sea, presumed drowned, and will then return to life, full of messages and miracles. The plot works well enough until the revival meeting, when people in attendance storm the stage, demanding to be healed, as Daisy Fay narrates: "Daddy always told me that Christians were dangerous and I believed him, so I picked up my choir robe and started running. Miss Irma Jean Slawson must have gone crazy, too, because at this point she began to play 'If I Knew You Were Coming, I'da Baked a Cake' that isn't even a religious number" (180). Slapstick like this cannot hide the deeper anger at men (and other than a few references to Tammy Faye Baker, they all are men) who take advantage of women in several ways: first, as financial losers in the guilt game and, second, as forced—in Daisy Fay's case—co-conspirators in the con game.

In current fiction, it seems that sincere preachers fare no better than false ones. Anne Tyler's novels are filled with ineffectual preachers, trapped preachers' wives, and suffering preachers' children, the satire so dominant in her writing that it defines and illustrates one of her major themes— change—as Elizabeth Evans has noted: "If change is to come, it must come from within the individual, not through the imposition of someone else's influence," namely organized religion.[9] Although Evans' book on Tyler has a short section on ministers in which she discusses the humorous preachers in *Searching for Caleb, The Clock Winder,* and *A Slipping-Down Life,* other novels by Tyler also contain satire about preachers and deserve some brief attention. In *Earthly Possessions,* the protagonist, Charlotte, is married to Saul, who abruptly announces one day that he has been saved and called to preach. In desperation, Charlotte tries to persuade him that his "vision" might only be "leftover sound waves or something," but her argument has no effect. In a passage representative of many of Tyler's characters who feel the constraints of religion, Charlotte thinks: "Although I didn't believe in God, I could almost change my mind now and imagine one, for who else would play such a joke on me? The only place more closed-in than this house was a church. The only person odder than my mother was a hellfire preacher. I nearly laughed" (*EP,* 95–96).

Throughout the novel, Charlotte feels confined—both physically (in her parents' house, her husband's house, the church, her kidnapper's car)

<hr>

9. Elizabeth Evans, *Anne Tyler* (New York, 1993), 74.

and psychologically (by her parents' rules, her marriage, religion's constraints, her kidnapper's control). Because religion and her husband are linked so closely, however, this combination becomes the dominant conflict in Charlotte's life and the major focus of her escape. Much of the humor in *Earthly Possessions* results from the constant yet subtle religious conflict between Charlotte and Saul. One problem Charlotte has with organized religion is that she does not believe anyone has a right to change other people, an opinion Tyler shares. As she stated in an interview with Wendy Lamb, Tyler is "particularly concerned with how much right anyone has to change someone, and ministers are people who feel they have that right."[10] Charlotte continues to resist religion throughout the novel, making sarcastic comments about Christianity and its promoters. When she sees a pamphlet entitled "What If Christ Had Never Come," she thinks, "I can think of a lot we'd have missed if Christ had never come. The Spanish Inquisition, for one thing. For another, losing my husband to the Hamden Bible College." This comment sums up much of Charlotte's religious antagonism; in fact, she sees herself as competing with God and Saul.

Added to this dual foe of God and husband is the issue, once again, of sex—as Charlotte attempts to separate Saul from God as a way of lessening the power both have over her life. Although Charlotte attends her husband's services, she spends the time daydreaming about how she can improve her chances for "winning," using sex as a weapon. She admits, "I plotted how to get him into bed with me. There was something magical about that pew that sent all my thoughts swooning toward bed. Contrariness, I suppose. He was against making love on a Sunday. I was in favor of it. Sometimes I won, sometimes he won. I wouldn't have missed Sunday for the world" (*EP,* 122–24). Saul's passion for religion is pitted against his passion for Charlotte, and she forces him to choose one or the other on Sunday afternoons; Charlotte wins against both God and husband, the two major powers in her life, if she convinces Saul to make love.

In addition, Charlotte believes Saul has given up independent thought, having had all decisions made for him by the tenets of the church—another dangerous pitfall of organized religion. She comments: "Oh, I did lose him. He wasn't the old Saul Emory. He'd adopted a whole new set of rules, attitudes, platitudes, judgments; he didn't even need to think. In any situation, all he had to do was rest back on his easy answers. He could reach for his religion and pull it around him like his preacher's robe" (*EP,* 122). Tyler suggests in this passage what many women authors believe: this religious at-

---

10. Wendy Lamb, "An Interview with Anne Tyler," in *Critical Essays on Anne Tyler,* ed. Alice Hall Petry (New York, 1992), 55.

titude is dangerous because it encourages unthinking acceptance of traditions, religious or otherwise. Tyler makes it clear that acceptance of any belief, social structure, or tradition without careful thought and analysis is detrimental to individuals and to society as a whole.

Not until Tyler's twelfth novel, *Saint Maybe,* is a preacher given honorable characteristics, appearing something other than absurd, although there is still much satire in this novel. Ian Bedloe's church is named The Church of the Second Chance, which has such rules as the Caffeine Rule, the Sugar Rule, and the Alcohol Rule, all of which are eventually exposed as futile and meaningless. What makes Ian different from Tyler's other preachers, though, is his sincerity. He lives a "Christian" life, not just in name but in spirit—by loving others and sacrificing himself for their benefit. The message Tyler proposes may be found in the title: Is Ian a Saint? Maybe. Then again, Ian might have been a good man without ever finding The Church of the Second Chance. Perhaps Ian's change comes from inside rather than from the church, something external—an idea more in keeping with Tyler's personal philosophy.

Although the South is predominantly Protestant, satire on Catholicism is surprisingly common in contemporary southern fiction, perhaps because of the Catholic Church's strong patriarchal structure and the asexuality of nuns. Sheila Bosworth, born and raised in New Orleans, a city she says "is maybe the only city in America that is run by Catholics," claims that Catholicism has "cost [her] a lot" and that she "was frightened to death as a child" by "mean nuns." Even though she admits Catholicism is "like breathing or eating" for her, her novels question, sometimes quite bitterly, its validity and applicability in the lives of her characters, in addition to examining its destructive and constructive force in people's lives.[11]

Both of Sheila Bosworth's novels to date are set in the New Orleans area, and her characters typically attend parochial schools run by discipline-minded nuns, much as Bosworth did as a child. More concerned with saving wood than souls, Bosworth's nuns patrol the classrooms and the church with vigilance, searching for sinners against property rather than against humanity. One character in *Slow Poison* notes: "Defacing the wood of school desks and church pews angered the Sisters of Mercy to a frenzy that appeared to be almost beyond their control. Maybe because Jesus was a carpenter" (*SP,* 50). In that novel, Bosworth satirically describes Sister Marcella, to whom punctuality is a sign of true goodness: "Sister Marcella didn't particularly care if you defaced wood, but she did hate the rail-

---

11. Bosworth, quoted in Ketchin, *Christ-Haunted Landscape,* 147, 148, 151.

clingers and the unpunctual. Two years ago, she had been pushed over the edge of tolerance by a class of seven-year-olds who had apparently refused to seize their parents' car keys and drive themselves to school at dawn" (71). This passage exposes the tendency some nuns have to separate themselves from reality, thereby losing touch with what real people must encounter each day. In addition, nuns are not confronted with the conflicts many women face over career, marriage, family, money, and gender respect. They have accepted their place in the Catholic hierarchy, leaving no battle to be fought. For this reason more than any other, they are viable targets for satire.

Satirizing both Catholics and Protestants, Valerie Sayers, whose *Who Do You Love?* is set in the fictional town of Due East, South Carolina, focuses on an Irish Catholic family, the Rooneys, who are both cultural and religious outsiders. In their attempts to gain respect from their Protestant neighbors, the Rooney children are taught to "stick their chests out and strut when it came to being Catholic: it was the only way to survive in a place where the other kids called you mackerel snapper and asked you were the nuns bald under those habits."[12] One character tells a joke about a Catholic girl who moves to the big city and becomes a prostitute when all other options fail. Returning home to visit, she sees her mother's face and bursts into tears:

> "What is it?" says her mother. "It can't be that bad now."
> "Oh, Mother," says the girl. "Oh, it's very bad indeed. I've become a prostitute." And she wails louder than before.
> Her mother turns gray as ash. "Sweet suffering mother of Jesus," she says. "Tell me, daughter, that I didn't hear you right."
> The girl is keening into the night. "It's true, Mother, it's true. I was starving and I became a *prostitute.*"
> Immediately the mother bursts into a merry laugh and pulls her daughter close. "Is that all?" she says. "You had me very worried there, my darling girl. I thought you said you'd become a *Protestant.*" (117–18)

Here, Sayers' satire strikes in both directions: She makes fun of Protestants—who are worse than prostitutes, according to the mother—and also of Catholics—who have an overdeveloped sense of their own superiority. This ability to laugh at one's own religion as well as others' marks her humor as particularly female. Traditionally, women's humor has been self-

12. Valerie Sayers, *Who Do You Love?* (1991; rpr. New York, 1992), 128.

deprecating, but modern southern women have learned that it is acceptable to laugh at others as well, and to admit that there is a bit of absurdity in everyone and in every institution.

Many women writers link this sense of absurdity with religious doubt, even though most of the authors in this study have Christian backgrounds, and most profess to some degree of faith in the existence of God.[13] But their work portrays a general doubt about God's effectiveness in the modern world. Bosworth, for example, has commented on her ambivalence about God: "I resented babies being hurt, and for what purpose? And suddenly in the 1970s the church was saying 'God is Love.' Well, that wasn't what we were taught; we were taught that God will love you if you were good. I mean God's love is universal but you got the impression that you yourself were pretty worthless."[14]

Lee Smith admits her inability to combine the spiritual with the mundane: "You know, I can't be transported. I have to go to the grocery store. . . . I can't have a religious experience; I have to be back by three. All these people are depending on me." Instead, she finds meaning in her work, which is "a sort of saving thing. Almost a religion of its own." And although Doris Betts claims she "cling[s] to the church," she also admits in her novels that she asks "those old questions—if there is a benevolent God, why is there so much evil and suffering in the world? Why does God allow the innocent to suffer?" answering with her "usual ambiguous answers at the end."[15] Doubt reveals itself through these authors' characters, who are often skeptical and cynical about religion and God. One of Brown's characters proclaims, "I used to think the beauty of Christianity is that no one is in danger of practicing it" (*B*, 315), and a character in Smith's *Black Mountain Breakdown* says, "I put Jesus in the same category as penicillin . . . and there's some that's allergic to both" (*MB*, 119).

One complaint against the Christian God that surfaces in women's writings is his lack of fairness and accountability, and these women's protests find him deficient in his maleness as well as in his divinity. In a region where the inhabitants feel they have been judged unfairly by nonsouthern-

---

13. Many of the writers in this study grew up in environments with strong Christian ties, for example, Doris Betts, whose family attended the Associate Reformed Presbyterian Church. She remembers reading the Bible as one of her first literary experiences. Lee Smith attended a private Episcopalian school. Gail Godwin attended a school run by a French order of nuns and was raised by a mother who was a devout Episcopalian. Anne Tyler's family spent time in an experimental Quaker community. Jill McCorkle was raised as a Southern Baptist, and Alice Walker credits her spirituality to the Bible and the blues.

14. Bosworth, quoted in Ketchin, *Christ-Haunted Landscape,* 151.

15. Smith and Betts quoted *ibid.,* 48, 51, 258, 240.

ers for a variety of "sins," these writers seem to feel that God, at least, should be just and follow rules of behavior similar to those of southern chivalry, as explained by Rory in *Slow Poison:* "Rory had written off St. Jude, but in 1967 she still held a belief in certain gentleman's rules for the Creator, a certain cosmic code of ethics. She still believed that tragedy confers transitory immunity from further tragedy, that trouble intrinsically, if temporarily, precludes more trouble. Thus, a nursing mother won't develop breast cancer. Loved ones don't drop dead at another loved one's funeral. A victim of acute appendicitis is not subject to menstrual cramps" (*SP,* 171).

Irony is rampant in novels such as this one. So much in life is unfair, it seems that a powerful God, at the very least, would operate according to a fair system. Ironic humor abounds in the questions characters ask either explicitly or implicitly. In *Pigs in Heaven,* for example, Barbara Kingsolver reveals that "Harland's sister got killed listening to 'Jesus Loves You This Morning' on the radio in her bathtub,"[16] and in one of Fannie Flagg's novels, the Whistle Stop Baptist Church Ladies' Bible Study Group has as its discussion topic, "Why Did Noah Let Two Snakes on the Boat When He Had a Chance to Get Rid of Them Once and for All?" (*FGT,* 77). Such ironies and inconsistencies in God's world are comic, but there is also a more serious questioning going on about meaning and order in God's plan. If God is a gentleman, he should follow a code of conduct. But he doesn't, and that makes these authors question his existence and purpose.

When ironic and seemingly unfair things do happen in fiction, as they do in life, many characters become disillusioned with God. Rita Mae Brown uses perhaps the most Juvenalian religious satire, and her characters seem especially prone to disillusionment, expressing such sentiments as, "God can't be all that great—everything he makes dies" (*SO,* 82). Much of Brown's satire is at the expense of the few believers in her novels—who are usually portrayed as fervent but misled. One such believer is Louise Hunsenmeir, who is much tormented by infidels around her, as in the scene in *Six of One* in which she is teasingly told that Easter would be canceled because they "found the body" (271). In *Venus Envy,* Brown includes a dream/vision sequence in which the protagonist, Frazier, goes to Mount Olympus and discusses religion with the gods. When she questions Venus and Mercury about the Christian God, the description they give is not flattering:

"He's so jealous. 'Thou shalt have no other gods before me.' You know, I faxed him the Ten Commandments a couple of years ago

16. Barbara Kingsolver, *Pigs in Heaven* (New York, 1993), 182.

with comments in the margins. He was livid. No sense of humor, that one. Wants everyone to feel guilty and ashamed."

"Hates women." Venus lay back on a pillow, her arms behind her head.

"Hates sex," Mercury grumbled. "I don't know why so many of you down there pay attention to him. He's quite hateful and cruel." (*VE*, 321–22)

In passages such as this, women writers question the reasoning behind God's actions, and in response, their characters are often able to come to some conclusions—however unflattering to the traditional Christian structure—or they learn to live with the ambiguity, unlike many of the characters in novels by male writers, who often end up suffering existential despair and angst, as Doris Betts explains: "Women in general have a tendency, if not to solve the problem, then at least to solve the nature of the person who has to live with it. That's very female, because women have never been able to pick up and just leave their problems behind. Either they go off to the asylum or they stay home and feed that baby, tend that old woman, wash that dead body. They don't go to sea or the French foreign legion. Coping produces a different attitude." Is this "attitude" faith? Perhaps. By Betts's definition, faith is "simply my decision to proceed in a certain direction."[17] If this is not a traditional definition of faith, it is because life now requires a different definition altogether, one that is pragmatic, one that works for women.

A character in Vicki Covington's *Gathering Home* prays with his social security number, addressing God with, "Hi. It's me, 422–87–9043" (205). In this passage, juxtaposing the ancient and sacred—prayer—with the modern—a social security number—is a way of questioning just how far religion can be modified for postmodern life without making it ineffective, meaningless, or ludicrous. In many novels, this juxtapositioning occurs during church plays, where there is a contradiction between the play and its players—between a solemn reenactment of a sacred moment and the high-spirited, modern characters acting out that moment. In the Christmas parade described in McCorkle's *Ferris Beach,* the "high school drama students who were manning the float had *live* animals, and now Joseph had thrown down his walking stick and was wrestling a sheep who was butting the chicken wire that enclosed the flatbed trailer" (*FB,* 117). And in another Christmas play in Brown's *Rubyfruit Jungle,* Molly (playing Mary) and

17. Quoted in Ketchin, *Christ-Haunted Landscape,* 252–53, 256.

Cheryl (playing Joseph) get into a war over who gets to speak the most lines. After they exchange ad lib remarks and drop the Jesus doll on the floor, their competition escalates to childhood frenzy:

> Well, Leroy was near to dying of perplexity and he started to say something too, but Cheryl cut him off with, "Don't worry, Mary, babies fall out of the cradle all the time." That wasn't enough for greedy-guts, she then goes on about how she was a carpenter in a foreign land and how we had to travel many miles just so I could have my baby. . . . I couldn't stand it any longer so I blurted out in the middle of her tale about the tax collectors, "Joseph, you shut up or you'll wake the baby." . . . As soon as I told Joseph to shut up, Miss Potter pushed the shepherds on the stage. . . . Just then Barry Aldridge, another shepherd, peed right there on the stage he was so scared. Joseph saw her chance and said in an imperious voice, "You can't pee in front of little Lord Jesus, go back to the hills." That made me mad. "He can pee where he wants to, this is a stable, ain't it?" (*RJ,* 46–47)

The exchange continues until Joseph/Cheryl is shoved into the audience, and Miss Potter gives up any hope of saving the show, ordering the audience to sing hymns instead, a "safe" activity, she believes, in any setting—ancient or modern.

Determining the boundary between modernizing Christianity by synthesizing it into contemporary society and destroying the intent of the religion by making it appear absurd is what leads to much satiric humor, again illustrated in *Ferris Beach,* in which Kate Burns describes her town's dramatic attempt to adapt religion to contemporary life: "*Jesus Christ Superstar* wasn't good enough; these people were set on writing their own opera that weekend. The climax came when Jesus went up to the Woman at the Well and sang 'Hello, I Love You'; somehow it didn't seem to be what either Jesus or Jim Morrison had intended" (*FB,* 46). In another scene, Kate describes the "modernization" she and her friend Misty give to church hymns, proving that this activity is not always "safe": "Whenever my mother allowed me to sit with Misty in church, we played a game where we'd close our eyes, open the hymnal, and then read the two titles with an ending of 'in the bed,' such as 'Just As I Am *in the bed*' or 'How Great Thou Art *in the bed*'" (126). While this first appears as just a silly child's game to pass time in church, it subtly suggests that religion often seems unsuitable or out of place when juxtaposed with modern life, as in West's *She Flew the Coop,* in which a church announces on its marquee, "1 FREE TRIP TO HEAVEN

DETAILS INSIDE!" (172) and the preacher describes heaven as a place where "there's air conditioning" (187).

On the topic of church drama, the novels of Rita Mae Brown are the most bitter, as noted earlier. In one conversation between characters betting on what will go wrong in the annual town parade, the line between satire and blasphemy blurs:

> "If only I could bet on Yashew Gregorivitch, but he's off the floats this year." Ramelle thought out loud.
> "Well, I guess after that scandal last year."
> "We never will see the equal of it."
> "The Dorcas Aid Society still won't speak to his mother. La Sermonetta prayed for his soul publicly lest the Lord strike him dead for portraying gentle Jesus on the cross."
> "I didn't mind him hanging on that cross with paint on his hands and feet, but the screaming was hard to bear."
> "I thought the float number on his back rather a nice touch."
> (*SO*, 42)

This scene comes brutally close to offending what many Americans deem sacrosanct, as Juvenalian satire often does. There are many, no doubt, who would not laugh at Brown's scene, just as there were many who did not laugh at Jonathan Swift's "A Modest Proposal." Brown and Swift, like other writers, ask difficult questions of society—questions that are nonetheless legitimate—even at the risk of offending people.

Closely tied at times to religious satire is satire aimed at sexuality. Lee Smith claims that in life there is "getting saved, sex, and writing. Those are the only things I know of," and while this may or may not be true, men have been privy to this female attitude toward sex only in the last generation.[18] Sexual humor has long been shared and appreciated by women in the company of other women—a sort of "kitchen" humor—but with the sexual revolution, women have started to share what they think is funny about sex. According to Rayna Green, southern women have kept their bawdy humor a secret so long because the image conflicts with the mythology of the southern lady as naïve and undefiled; by coming out of the kitchen, women are signaling they can no longer live with such stereotypes. When a woman makes a sexual joke, she acknowledges that she is "fallen"—that is, she admits she has a knowledge of sex. Traditionally, Good Girls are sexually pure and therefore do not understand or make sex-

18. Quoted *ibid.*, 51.

ual jokes, but by combining the images of the Good Girl and the Bad Girl in the same character, women are allowing themselves to express honest feelings about sex without fearing loss of respect.

Anne Jones believes that women's open humor about sex is directly related to a woman's control of her own body; women can diminish a man's phallic power symbolically by diminishing the penis, which is often but not always the target of women's sexual humor. Laughing at a man's body, Jones asserts, is a way for women to laugh at "not only men's claims to power but the fantasy of power itself." Regina Barreca also considers sexual jokes a matter of power, claiming that men "worry that when we get together we talk about our lovers. This is a good worry. This is worry with some substance behind it," especially when the topic is ex-lovers, because it is "a way of regaining a sense of control."[19] In a society that has tried to convince white women to remain frigid on a pedestal, sexual rebellion is especially culturally disruptive and troubling to some men.

Satire, then, is the most popular fictional mode for exploring sex, relationships, and power. The southern woman, previously the power and influence behind the man, is assuming full control over self and relationships, in some cases even subjugating the man, as two nurses illustrate in Alther's *Other Women:* "Yeah, we were watching Arlene give a bed bath, weren't we? And she said if a male patient got an erection, to hit it with a spoon" (170). Literally an incident of "male bashing," this scene shows women taking power for themselves by incapacitating the phallic power. Usurping power can also be done verbally, as the women in a Florence King novel do by making fun of the unfortunately named lawyer Richard Pinckney Farnsworth, Jr., nicknamed "Little Dick" (*FSL*, 106).

There are not very many examples of happy relationships in contemporary southern fiction by male or female authors. One difference from the female perspective is that relationships and sex are more often handled humorously and ironically. Women writers are also exploring exclusively female topics previously ignored or glossed over by male authors—such as the female orgasm—and women are clearly shown as active sexual beings.

Learning about sex is an area rich in pathos as well as humor because of the lack of education many southern girls receive. In yet another link between religion and sex, Lillian Smith theorizes that religion has denied women knowledge about their sexuality in order to maintain patriarchal control: "I have at moments wondered if moralists had only morals at heart or if they had also the self-esteem of little males in mind when they hid from children the facts of life, fearing perhaps that little females might

19. Jones, "Incredible," 471; Barreca, *They Used to Call me Snow White,* 153.

over-value their role in this drama of creation and, turning 'uppity' as we say in Dixie, forget their inferior place in the scheme of things."[20] Smith's statement would imply, then, that gaining and expressing sexual knowledge is cultural and religious rebellion, a way for women to fight their subordinate position in the religious and social hierarchy.

From trying to get accurate information about sex to learning where to put their hands during intercourse, young southern girls in contemporary novels struggle through sexual initiation, learning to laugh at the sometimes ridiculous situations sex creates. In Sayers' *Who Do You Love?* eleven-year-old Kate is curious about sex but will not ask her mother because she is sure her mother is "interested in books and politics and music and poetry: not the function of genitals"; ironically, her mother waits patiently, sure Kate will ask her questions as soon as she becomes interested in the subject of sex. Instead, Kate embarks on a self-taught course, randomly finding words in the dictionary in an absurd circuitous search for sexual knowledge: "Since September, when they'd moved the sixth grade to the junior high school, Kate Rooney had stepped up the dictionary word searches and had long since gone beyond guide words. She'd found *intercourse, intercourse* meant *copulation* and *copulation* meant *coitus* and *coitus* meant *intercourse*," leaving her back where she started and still confused (*W,* 13). Florence King has no better luck, remaining "unaware of erection, penetration, and ejaculation," believing "that a dangling participle was placed on a split infinitive and that was that" (*FSL,* 114). In Smith's *Black Mountain Breakdown,* the authoritative information Crystal Spangler gets is even less helpful and less accurate than Kate Rooney's dictionary searches. She is instructed at a Methodist Youth Fellowship meeting in the old traditions of male and female sexual responsibility that support the male-dominated religion: "One night their leader, Mrs. Robert Haskell, tells the girls of the MYF never to pet, because boys can become so excited during the act of petting that they can literally *die* if they don't have a chance to relieve themselves. Girls have more control, of course, so girls are responsible for seeing that petting does not occur. The girls of the MYF nod seriously. Life-and-death decisions are safe with them" (*BMB,* 139). Such information is given in good faith by misled but well-meaning adult characters, but the results are a generation of misinformed females who spend the rest of their lives trying to separate fact from fiction, as well as fearing the uncontrollable sexual urges of the opposite sex, who are unfairly presented as creatures driven by their instincts who, once aroused, must choose between committing rape and dying.

20. Smith, *Killers of the Dream,* 88.

With accurate information from tolerant adults, much of the embarrassment stemming from adolescent ignorance could be avoided—including embarrassment to the adults when their "lies" are exposed. In Boyd's *The Revolution of Little Girls,* Ellen Burns is taken to the gynecologist when she is only nine years old because her "vaginal discharge," brought on naturally as she reads a stimulating book about sex, is mistaken by her mother as an infection. Rather than preparing her young daughter by telling her exactly what to expect—that the procedure is awkward but necessary—Ellen's mother is too embarrassed and so only warns her that "the examination might hurt a little but that [she] should be brave." Everyone—the doctor, her mother, her aunt—seems embarrassed about the whole situation, and in an attempt to allay the awkward silence, misinformed Ellen only makes the situation worse:

> So when Dr. Post put a piece of cold metal inside me . . . I said, "It's okay, it doesn't hurt." He still looked sternly embarrassed. "It feels good, really."
>
> My mother was giving me her grimmest look.
>
> "It does feel good," I said to her, but she didn't look any happier, so I raised my head and leaned up on my elbows and laughed gaily over the sheet, looking at each of them in turn. "It tickles, really. It feels good. No problem." (*RLG,* 91)

Ellen's attempts a few years later to lose her virginity are equally doomed because of her mother's advice to wear a girdle at all times because *"Any woman looks better in a girdle."* But she also follows the advice of her friend who gives her a vaginal suppository that is "supposed to lubricate [her]." Deciding midway through the date that the girdle will get in the way of anything her date has in mind, she finally decides, "The girdle meant I couldn't make love, but the suppository meant I sincerely wanted to" (*RLG,* 51).

Far from the monumental and earth-moving experiences found in romantic novels, sex is often found by fictional southern girls to be confusing and comic. Ginny Babcock in *Kinflicks* describes her first sexual encounter in amusing but disappointing terms: "Frankly, the rupturing of my maidenhead had been just about as meaningful as the breaking of a paper Saniband on a motel toilet," and she further laments sarcastically, "Poor Mother, she had failed to capture yet another of my golden firsts with her Kodak M24 Instamatic" (*K,* 130). Such ironic commentary on the "big moment" puts sex in realistic perspective, deromanticizing the sex act as less than the wondrous and magical event young girls imagine.

In *A Room of One's Own,* Virginia Woolf argues that women "have served all these centuries as looking-glasses possessing the magic and delicious power of reflecting the figure of man at twice its natural size," and that once women begin "to tell the truth, the figure in the looking-glass shrinks."[21] It may be fair to say that contemporary southern women writers are holding up the looking-glass and seeing themselves as well, for it is not only men in these passages who are shrinking through accurate reflection. Not just fathers and male religious leaders are at fault for withholding knowledge and therefore power. These authors expose how women, too—mothers, friends, female religious leaders—contribute to the lack of information and therefore the subjugation of little girls and grown women. If men have sexual information and women do not, women will be at a disadvantage in every way in relationships, depending on men to lead and guide them.

Lack of information is just one of the criticisms women writers offer in their depiction of sex, especially sex in marriage. A critical eye toward marriage is nothing new in American literature, of course. Many writers, among them William Dean Howells, Edith Wharton, Ellen Glasgow, and John Updike, have been extremely judgmental of marriage, but what is new is the boldness in the female perspective, exposing the follies of the institution itself, the sex act, and many times the inept male partners involved, questioning to what extent marriage is necessary or viable in our society today. One of Rita Mae Brown's characters, for example, asks, "Why get married? It's easier to hang myself" (*VE,* 113).

Problems with marriage are not limited to the male sex, but because women have been trained for so long to accept patriarchal leadership in the home, and because men have been taught that to be men they must wield a firm hand, the men often end up looking like tyrants. Men more often use force, both physical and psychological, to get what they want, as opposed to women, who more often use humor. The father in Ansa's *Ugly Ways* had at one time been a brutal man: demanding, inflexible, and physically violent. In "the battle that had been their marriage," husband was pitted against wife in a struggle for power, the difference being that the husband's "attacks" were obvious and visible whereas the wife's were subtle and passively aggressive, as well as very often comic in nature. He would order her to clean his boots, he would rap on his empty plate when he wanted more food, and he would make her "take a mayonnaise jar along on a car trip for her to pee in so they wouldn't have to stop along the road." In response, she would "forget" to clean the boots, she would serve him an "okra holo-

21. Virginia Woolf, *A Room of One's Own* (1929; rpr. San Diego, 1989), 35–36.

caust," and she would call him "Mr. Bastard" to her friends and family behind his back (*UW,* 126–28). Although her methods are comic, it is a comedy of rage, one of the only strategies available to oppressed women.

Such passive-aggressive behavior by women is one of the few defenses against the overwhelming power, physical and cultural, that some men assume. In *Almost Innocent,* Aunt Mathilde tries to convince her husband to pick up his clothes by "hiding all clothing which she found draped over the bedpost or flung across chairs; when he didn't look for the missing items, or even inquire as to their whereabouts, she began giving them away, piece by piece. One day, Uncle Howard caught Shenandoah, his yardman, in Magazine Street Hardware wearing a red quilted smoking jacket emblazoned with Howard's monogram. By the next day, both Shenandoah and [the] uncle were gone, although no one supposed they had become traveling companions" (*AI,* 87). This comic episode shows readers that the fault with marriage cannot be assigned to the male or to the female so much as to lack of communication, and the blame for that is not easy to assign. Cultural expectations, gender stereotypes, and popular culture are just some of the influences that keep partners from expressing honest thoughts and emotions and make them do what they think they are supposed to do.

Nowhere is this better illustrated than in the sex life of Ginny and Ira in *Kinflicks.* Ira is sure that he and Ginny will not be happily married until she experiences an orgasm, and Ginny reports the sad and funny schedule he imposes on them in an attempt to achieve this goal: "Much more crucial to the health of our marriage than our ensuing record of church attendance was the fact that our next 172 attempts at intercourse were dismal, from Ira's point of view. They were easy to count because we made love every Monday, Wednesday, and Friday night. Ira had read in the *Reader's Digest* that the average American couple had sex twice a week. Hence we would have it three times a week. . . . He wrote it in on the kitchen calendar in red pencil each week so that we would be sure not to forget it" (*K,* 379–80). This kind of imposed pressure, of course, goes against Ira's goal, and eventually Ginny fakes an orgasm on their first anniversary "after fifty-eight minutes of excessively imaginative foreplay and approximately 212 thrusts" (382). What makes this a comic scene are some of the same things that characterize it as "southern": the concrete and detailed description, the exaggeration (the reader hopes), and the detached sense of humor.

To be fair to both sexes, Ellen Gilchrist puts a comic twist on the woman-faking-orgasm stereotype in *Starcarbon,* a novel about the troubled love affairs among various couples. One couple, Georgia and Zach, has many problems, including Zach's occasional impotence when he becomes distracted by social injustices. Georgia eventually leaves him, saying, "The last straw was when you started faking orgasms while being fellated."[22] Absurd (and hard to imagine), this passage makes the point that men also feel tremendous pressure in sexual situations and wonder just what is required of them to participate in a successful relationship.

Some of the unhappiness and dissatisfaction in love and sex in these novels can be blamed on stereotypes and myths; it is interesting and significant how often characters refer to movies and novels as the source of romantic expectations. Ruby Pitt Woodrow in Gibbons' *A Virtuous Woman* cries as she leaves for her honeymoon, commenting with both optimism and anger, "I thought time would take care of me, that once we had our rings and a nice honeymoon hotel that everything would be just fine. I'd call daddy and we'd chat just like Elizabeth Taylor and Spencer Tracy in *Father of the Bride,* one of those daydreamy movies that had contributed to the mess I was in" (29). Romantic movies, myths, and fairytales take a real beating in contemporary southern novels by women. In Betts's *Heading West,* Chan Thatcher has discarded all her illusions about love. She comments, "Penelope's behavior, she was certain, had been invented by a male author with greater optimistic ego than powers of observation" (*HW,* 180), and later admits, "I've always thought that when the Prince kissed Sleeping Beauty she probably said, 'Move out of my way,' and took off," a comment that a male character aptly labels "feminist revision" (189).

As Sandra M. Gilbert and Susan Gubar have argued, fairytales and myths can be especially debilitating to the independence and growth of girls and women because they "state and enforce culture's sentences with greater accuracy than more sophisticated texts."[23] Such stories perpetuate the Scarlett/Melanie polarity, reinforcing traditional gender roles by teaching women to be childlike, submissive, and silent—as well as supporting the stereotype of Woman as Prize. By "revisioning" fairytales in their novels, these writers clear space for women to be more than a princess or a witch.

In comparison to the romantic illusions propagated by popular culture and fairytales, sex in southern novels is sometimes startling, not because of the explicitness but because of the realism. There are very few moments of transcendence and splendor, and more moments of realistic and cynical observations, such as the remark by Jo Spencer in *The Cheer Leader:* "I also see that being in love and being dumb are often simultaneous actions" (27). Brown's *Southern Discomfort* contains much blatant humor about sex, usually in the form of jokes told by witty prostitutes at the expense of their cus-

---

22. Ellen Gilchrist, *Starcarbon* (New York, 1994), 64.

23. Sandra M. Gilbert and Susan Gubar, *The Madwoman in the Attic: The Woman Writer and the Nineteenth-Century Literary Imagination* (New Haven, 1979), 36–40.

tomers. Doubly marginalized as women and prostitutes, these women refuse to accept the restrictions society has placed on them because of their profession, combating society's structure with humor as a way of maintaining their identity and sanity. Men—who are at once their support and their downfall—are most often portrayed as insensitive and egotistical, generally serving as the target for their jokes. Although her perspective may be distressing to some men, Brown is only asking for equal time. Jokes stereotyping women—especially white women in the South—as frigid, inhibited, and uninterested in sex, have dominated literature and life, and Brown takes equal shots in fun, focusing on the female side of sex for prostitutes, which is sometimes not very much fun, as in one woman's response to the song "Someday My Prince Will Come": "Yeah, in your mouth" (*SD,* 76). Brown, moreover, is following Virginia Woolf's advice "to laugh, without bitterness, at the vanities . . . of the other sex. For there is a spot the size of a shilling at the back of the head which one can never see for oneself. . . . A true picture of man as a whole can never be painted until a woman has described that spot the size of a shilling."[24]

Even though most of the males in Brown's novel are less than honorable, her female characters do not hate men. Unfortunately, jokes like those Brown's characters make have led some critics to misinterpret how women feel about sex and men. If men make jokes about sex, as they often do, does it mean they hate women? Probably not, and yet this misconception is often applied to women writers who make jokes about men. The growth in lesbian literature has led to some interesting, misinformed, and stereotypical comments about just this idea. Frederick Karl states in *American Fictions* that women characters in contemporary novels often attempt to "drown" the men in their lives, breaking free "often into a lesbian relationship, or into another cycle of dependency, sometimes in doom." He describes a pattern: "This pattern becomes paradigmatic: the need to break away in order to survive; defensiveness toward men, the sense of being taken, the consciousness that men will always triumph on their terms; the growing loyalties to women's movements, and with this, the movement toward lesbian relationships."[25]

Karl makes several implicit errors in logic in this statement. First, he implies that lesbianism arises out of anger against men, a point clearly denied in the fiction represented in this study, in which lesbianism is more often a conscious choice or an inherent disposition rather than a last resort. In novels with lesbian or bisexual characters—for example, those by Rita Mae

24. Woolf, *Room of One's Own,* 90–91.
25. Frederick R. Karl, *American Fictions, 1940–1980* (New York, 1983), 421, 424.

Brown, Lisa Alther, and Blanche McCrary Boyd—lesbianism is a decision made by women out of love for other women, not out of hatred for men. Second, Karl's statement seems to imply that lesbianism grew out of women's movements rather than having existed since ancient times. Attitudes like his lead some characters to conclude in despair, as does Boyd's lesbian character Ellen: "There were, I had decided, three categories in the world: men, women, and me" (*RLG,* 13).

Deromanticizing sex and determining just what is normal preoccupies many writers, leading to some very humorous scenes about nontraditional sex. By satirizing the aberrant desires of both men and women, writers ask exactly what is normal and acceptable in a modern sexual relationship. Many comic scenes revolve around strange fantasies of men that put women in the position of object rather than partner, creating satiric questioning of just how far a woman should have to go to be a "good sport." In *Six of One,* Pearlie asks to put rouge on his wife's nipples (*SO,* 177); in *Fancy Strut,* Ron asks Ruthie to put Chapstick on hers;[26] in *Who Do You Love?* Bill imagines dabbing "a little pecan pie filling onto the pale nipples" of the girl he will eventually marry; and in *Kinflicks,* Ira handcuffs both Ginny and himself over an oak beam and attempts to have sex while dangling from the rafter in yet another attempt to excite his wife to orgasm (393). Nowhere in these examples is there a concern for the woman's opinions or desires, yet it is assumed and hoped the male partner is interested in pleasing her. Although such scenes are funny, the humor is used to make a point about whether complicity should be expected, even demanded, in a sexual relationship.

There is a great deal of sex in contemporary novels by southern females, but there is very little sex in the traditional style, which poses some interesting questions about what is considered "normal" in a modern sexual relationship. Beverly Lowry's most recent novel, *The Track of Real Desires,* offers some entertaining answers. Set during one evening and night, the story centers on a dinner party to celebrate the return visit of Leland Standard to her hometown of Eunola, Mississippi. The final few chapters of the novel take place after dinner and are a montage of scenes involving people having sex, but not one couple is having sex in any traditional way: Totty only allows her husband, Dog, to enter her orally and anally, with the pain she experiences satisfying her punishment fantasies and convincing her she "was the girl she knew she had to be" (*RD,* 199). Mell asks her husband to wait until her sleeping pills take effect, which he does, never waking her while he satisfies himself. Carroll is presumably with his homosexual lover,

26. Lee Smith, *Fancy Strut* (1973; rpr. New York, 1991), 172.

Robin, but possibly not having sex since they "didn't always have sex, didn't always feel the need; they craved the holding more, the closeness, the contact" (212). Leland and Jacky spend the night together but never have intercourse; instead, they talk all night in different positions, "lying with her head at his feet, her feet in his armpits" and later "curled in a ball together" (207). Finally, Sissy speeds along the levee road, listening to opera on her tape deck while she masturbates, eventually wrecking the car and killing herself, making the final chapters a nicely constructed juxtapositioning of *eros* and *thanatos*. Such a conglomeration of unusual sexual scenes is both comic and tragic, and the satire of contemporary American sexual life is powerful. What is normal and what is abnormal today? The answer, at least according to Lowry, is that sexual prescription is impossible, challenging the belief that there is a "right" way of doing things.

With all the misconceptions and stereotypes, it is surprising that women in contemporary novels ever find good sex and feel free enough to enjoy it, but as with many obstacles put in the way of southern women, they have found a way to get around those barriers. In *Southern Discomfort,* even though the prostitutes are understandably cynical about love and sex, the hope for occasional satisfying connections with other human beings remains, and they express this hope the same way they express their other feelings—through humor:

> As Lottie selected onions, Rhonda absentmindedly peeled off some of the paper skin. "Hey, I heard a good one today. What do you get when you cross an onion with a donkey?"
>
> "What?" Lottie fell for it.
>
> "Most of the time you get an onion with big ears, but once in a great while you'll get a piece of ass that'll bring tears to your eyes." (*SD,* 201)

Generally, contemporary southern women writers are uninhibited concerning sex in their novels. Contrary to the image of the proper southern lady, in most cases the New Woman of the South is more tolerant of sexuality and its expression than ever before, although many believe that African American women in the South have always been that way. Lillian Smith has addressed what she believes to be the race differences in sexuality in *Killers of the Dream,* arguing that black women's sexual freedom results from a less restrictive religious and cultural background, creating a healthier sexual and mental life for African Americans. According to Smith, blacks have avoided the sexual anxieties whites endure because they have been "unconfused by a patriarchal-puritanic system which psychically castrated its women."[27]

The southern writer Reynolds Price concurs with Smith, explaining that African Americans gave the South many gifts, "the most paradoxical of all [being] . . . sexual health"; up against opposition of various kinds, "black men and women nonetheless continue to show white Southerners that the flesh itself, when honorably used, is a healing power." Smith's and Price's theories are echoed by Minrose Gwin, who argues that black women have long been seen by white women as "dark sides of their own sexual selves," suggesting a sexual liberation unavailable historically to white women. Finally, Toni Morrison claims that black women see themselves as sexually superior to white women, who are ignorant of facts and sexually repressed, and although this may be yet another stereotype contemporary white southern women are attempting to shatter, its power in the culture and its reflection in the literature is undeniable.[28]

The African American writer Dori Sanders includes sexual humor in conversations among aging, widowed women who lament their own lack of sex and the lack of understanding between the sexes in general. In *Her Own Place*, Ellabelle exclaims wistfully, "Just might snare me an old nighthawk. He'll be good for the night and can fly off in the morning. This old tired body could stand a little tune-up. My engine parts have been neglected too long."[29] In addition to breaking stereotypes about older women's openly expressed sexual desires, this remark by Ellabelle also surprises and delights because she is looking for a one-night fling rather than a long-term relationship.

Such sexual humor as this—by older women—has also been a sort of "kitchen humor," which Rayna Green claims has always existed, especially in the South: "The South, like many traditional cultures, offers an increase in license to those who advance in age, and those I have known take full advantage of it, delighting in presenting themselves as wicked old ladies."[30] The surprises continue in Sanders' novel as the women make comments incongruous with the myth of the proper older southern lady. Another character in the novel says, "I called up Mr. Clay Lewis one evening, and I said to him on the telephone, come on over. I'm a-sitting here all alone with

27. Smith, *Killers of the Dream*, 118.

28. Reynolds Price, *Clear Pictures: First Loves, First Guides* (New York, 1988), 107–108; Minrose C. Gwin, *Black and White Women of the Old South: The Peculiar Sisterhood in American Literature* (Knoxville, Tenn., 1985), 5; Toni Morrison, "What the Black Woman Asks About Woman's Lib," *New York Times Magazine*, August 22, 1971, p. 63.

29. Dori Sanders, *Her Own Place* (Chapel Hill, 1993), 113.

30. Green, "Magnolias," in *Speaking for Ourselves*, ed. Alexander, 23.

nothing on but my TV" (*HOP,* 116). Downplaying the power of men in relationships, the protagonist, Mae Lee, asks, "Why can't women learn that when it comes to marriage and sex, men are blind? Poor things, they only know how to eat what they are fed" (134–35).

Questioning traditional roles and values in religion and relationships through satire allows women to stand on equal ground with men in talking about real life. When one of Alther's characters relates the story of a prostitute whose client dies during sex, who then tells her doctor, "Well, Doc, I thought he was coming, but I guess he was going," one laughs at the absurdity of life, at sex, and at death. Lillian Smith says that in the Old South, southern white women "convinced themselves that God had ordained that they be deprived of pleasure," and sex "was pushed out through the back door as a shameful thing never to be mentioned" as a result of the strict religious tenets that feared the disruptive influence of the sexual Other.[31] Perhaps contemporary southern women writers are finally bringing sex back inside the house, this time through the front door.

31. Smith, *Killers of the Dream,* 141.

chapter five

The Hand Inside the Velvet Glove: Confronting Stereotypes

Southern women are Mack trucks disguised as powder puffs.
—REYNOLDS PRICE

No matter which sex I went to bed with, I never smoked on the street.
—FLORENCE KING

The South has gone through dramatic changes since the Civil War and even since Faulkner's time; economic growth, the civil rights movement, and the women's movement have all contributed to a South that is, on the whole, thriving, culturally diverse, and forward looking. But change has not come at the expense of history, for women writers have taken the best of the past and added the best of the present to create a new southern literature. The differences between the Old South and the contemporary South have created tension, however, that serves as the basis for a great deal of the conflict in southern fiction today. Not all dilemmas have been resolved, of course, nor can they be, but the questions about what should be preserved and what should be changed continue to be asked. As a character in Godwin's *The Odd Woman* observes, "All the old forms, at least the effortless practice of the old forms, [are] going out the window. Or maybe we'll have to rethink the reasons for them, and then find ourselves wanting to practice them again" (166).

To explore those conflicts between old and new forms, women writers often employ satire, and one topic especially amenable to satire is the role of women in the South. The stereotypes of southern women—both black and white—persist in reality and in fiction, limiting and pigeonholing women. And because these authors are writing the satire about themselves, there are really three perspectives they address: how the rest of the world sees southern women, how America sees southern women writers, and how southern women writers see themselves.

One myth that seems especially resistant to change is that of the southern belle. In the introduction to *The Female Tradition in Southern Literature,*

Carol Manning offers an explanation of why this image is so significant in women's writings: "Just as the male writer, and critic, might tend to be obsessed with the father and grandfather figures, so is it natural for the female writer to react particularly to the dominant female images—to the mother and the grandmother, yes, but especially to the Southern belle, the Southern lady, the enduring mammy—and to the society's expectations of Southern womanhood."[1]

Coming to terms with old stereotypes is necessary before new images can be established. This is certainly true for southern women, but it is also true for women in any region who attempt to combat stereotypes. Louis D. Rubin, Jr.'s concept of the Great American Joke—that American humor is based largely on the incongruity between the ideal and the real—has double meaning for women, as Nancy Walker explains: "Women's humor also deals with incongruity—with the contrast between the official mythology and the daily reality—but it . . . develops from a different premise: the world they inhabit is not of their making, and often not much to their liking, so their tactics must be those of survivors rather than those of saviors." Being a survivor in a society that still assumes a southern white woman should be virtuous, nurturing, and helpless, requires first acknowledging the past and its mythology and then reacting against it. Ignoring it will not reduce its hold on the consciousness of Americans, as Nina Baym argues: "The fact that a myth is a myth—that is, a falsehood—does not mean that it lacks power. And if it has power, then it has real—that is, material—effects."[2]

Women writers find the stereotype of the southern belle objectionable for several reasons. First, as Peggy Whitman Prenshaw points out, the image is damaging to the mind and life of every woman who lives in a society with such a stereotype held up as the ideal: "What stands revealed in this literature is the enormous psychic cost to women of a role absurdly inconsistent with life, and yet rigidly defined and extolled with religious fervor."[3] Most important, the stereotype is historically linked to slavery and racism. As Prenshaw and many others have shown, the image of the southern white woman as frail and weak has long been used to justify, first, the institution of slavery and, second, violence against black men as a means of protecting and serving her. As long as white women are helpless and black men and

---

1. Manning, ed., *Female Tradition*, 8.

2. See Louis D. Rubin, Jr.'s essay "The Great American Joke" in *The Comic Imagination in American Literature*, ed. Louis D. Rubin, Jr., (New Brunswick, N.J., 1973), 3–15; Walker, "*A Very Serious Thing*," 36; Nina Baym, "The Myth of the Myth of Southern Womanhood," *Feminism and American Literary History: Essays* (New Brunswick, N.J., 1992), 183.

3. Prenshaw, "Southern," in *Female Tradition*, ed. Manning, 80.

women are oppressed, the white patriarch remains in power. By challenging the myths surrounding southern womanhood, female writers challenge and criticize their passive role in the history of the South as well as the oppressive power of white men.

Kathryn Lee Seidel's *The Southern Belle in the American Novel* analyzes the role of the belle in fiction written between approximately 1830 and 1940. Seidel sees the belle as a "central metaphor" for the South: "the pure flower" of an "Edenic Garden" that "has been devastated by war and Reconstruction." The belle was placed on a pedestal because men made her the objective correlative for the ideals of the South. Of course, this image would be impossible for any living woman to exemplify, and in the early twentieth century, Seidel explains, "critical modern writers use the 'darker' side of the belle—the repressed narcissism, etc.—to indict the Old South or to describe the New." Seidel's theory helps explain characters like Faulkner's Temple Drake in *Sanctuary,* who is a victim of her upbringing as a southern belle because she has not been given the proper tools for survival in the modern world. Tragically, Temple (and other women like her) has been taught, according to Seidel, "to see herself as a beautiful object . . . and is not concerned with any talents that do not contribute to the goal her society has chosen for her: winning a man."[4]

Although readers may pity characters like Temple Drake, southern belles in contemporary literature are not absolved of their ignorance so easily. Thanks to the women's movement, the knowledge young women need is certainly available to them if they choose to acquire it, and those who do not become figures not of tragedy but of satire. The southern belle in contemporary literature may have become "a new stereotype, a cliché," as Seidel claims, but many authors have constructed and used this stereotype carefully and deliberately.[5] The belle is still a symbol of the Old South, but now she is also a symbol for the cultural obstacles standing in the way of progress for women, specifically, of the myth that southern white women are frail, uneducated, naïve, dependent, and sexually repressed.

Writers reacting satirically to this stereotype illustrate the absurdity and impracticality of maintaining such an image in the late twentieth century. Southern belles in contemporary fiction are almost always depicted as useless and absurd: image and style are all important; depth is rare. Such a woman is "serious about her hair as only Texan women can be serious about their hair" (*VE,* 200); they are "reckless belles . . . who show more

---

4. Kathryn Lee Seidel, *The Southern Belle in the American Novel* (Tampa, 1985), 50–51, xiv, 32.

5. *Ibid.,* 165.

style flying drunk through the windshield of a careening automobile than an ordinary woman can muster coming up the aisle on her wedding day" (*SP,* 97), and they are women afraid of nothing "except that it might rain on Mardi Gras" (176). Kaye Gibbons describes a belle in *A Cure for Dreams* as "Very superior. I'm sure when she died and entered heaven she asked to see the upstairs,"[6] and in Flagg's *Daisy Fay and the Miracle Man,* Daisy Fay is told that "the only two books in the world that really mean anything are the *Memphis Junior League Cookbook* and the Holy Bible, in that order" (54).

According to these authors, belles lead superficial lives, believing they are making a difference, but in truth, they are ignorant of the world, as Ellen Gilchrist describes in *Net of Jewels:* "Ladies spent the mornings getting dressed and the afternoons playing bridge. Whose intellectual food was the *Dunleith Daily* and the *Birmingham News* and the main selections of the Book-of-the-Month Club. Who thought New York City was where you went to spend the day at Elizabeth Arden and the evenings seeing Broadway musicals or carefully selected plays without any dirty language. Where everybody went to church and sent money to Africa to save the heathen but took it for granted that the black people in Dunleith couldn't read."[7]

These women might demand a certain respect, if for nothing else than their clinging tenaciously to a time and a style long outdated, but they live by a code of behavior that is unrealistic and implicitly racist. In McCorkle's *Ferris Beach,* Mrs. Poole is such a woman: "She was that misplaced woman who attempted to maintain aristocracy in a primarily blue-collar town. . . . She could see no merit in *any* changes, whether it was the Coca-Cola bottle getting taller or Mo Rhodes turning the yard of her split-level into a Japanese garden, or black children walking the halls of Samuel T. Saxon Junior High" (35). Resisting change in any form marks the belle as stubborn and fearful of differences, differences as innocuous as creative landscaping or as socially significant as integration. A belle ignorantly believes the way it has always been done is the best way, and by parodying social rules, women writers question the validity of maintaining those rules in contemporary life.

Indoctrination in the manners and style necessary to be a southern belle begins early for white girls in the South, and through young eyes, the traditions seem even more absurd. The two girls in *Ferris Beach* are forced to attend a meeting of the United Daughters of the Confederacy because they are officially members of the Children of the Confederacy. The girls observe while a pompous woman introduces herself by listing her ancestors

6. Kaye Gibbons, *A Cure for Dreams* (1991; rpr. New York, 1992), 95.
7. Ellen Gilchrist, *Net of Jewels* (New York, 1992), 48.

who served in the war, glossing over private and public scandals, and casually mentioning historical events like the Underground Railroad "as if it had just been built and she herself had tunneled her way beneath the streets of Boston." The girls stifle giggles when the speaker reports that her husband died of consumption, because Kate remembers her father's words on the subject: "I believe he died of consumption. . . . I know lots of men who were with him while he was consuming. He consumed a lot. He consumed so much that his nickname was Hooch" (*FB,* 123–24). Such satire underscores the absurdity of a social structure that refuses to distinguish between the ideal and the real, whether it concerns the accuracy of historical narratives such as in McCorkle's scene, or the disparity between the real and idealized southern woman.

As already mentioned, the stereotype of the southern belle is tied closely to race and social class in the South and is a form of elitism, an aspect that clearly angers many contemporary authors. Parents want daughters to fit the stereotype because it marks them as upper-class young women with social and marital potential; of course, this means that many young women are excluded. It is not surprising, then, to find a great deal of satire streaming from members of the middle and lower classes, such as Valerie Sayers' Kate Rooney, who describes the future belles in her school: "That giggle— now slurping, now soughing—acted on Kate as a prod. She heard that giggle every day in the halls of Due East Junior High School: the giggle of Southern belles in training, of future sorority sisters at Carolina. The giggle of a little *lady,* in her perfect cotton shirtdress" (*W,* 11).

There is a much more bitter tone in this satire than in McCorkle's, as would be expected because it comes from an excluded character, that tone escalating later in the novel when Kate describes these girls' activities as they grow older: "They tended the azaleas downtown for the Garden Club. They met the first Thursday of every month to discuss Mary Cassatt's sweet paintings or Emily Dickinson's sweet poems, and the *Courier* reported which of them officiated at the tea table. They sat in clusters on their verandas, gesturing with frosted glasses in their hands. . . . They were slender and breastless. They wore short little green golfing skirts, and bounding white pompons peeked out from the backs of their tennis shoes. . . . They were false simpering treacly mindless pandering sycophantic grown-up girls, and they got married to self-satisfied men who drove big white Cadillacs and let their bellies grow as big as their cars' V-8 engines" (*W,* 32). This passage begins with a mild description of activities that, while superficial, are harmless, but the tone of the satire becomes progressively stronger, angrier, and more accusatory. By the end of the paragraph, Sayers is not just attacking these women's meager attempts to fill their lives with meaningful activities. Adjectives such as "treacly," "pandering," and "sycophantic" connote self-serving manipulation, and the women are no longer depicted as innocent but as threatening and devious; the subtext of the passage warns one to be aware and wary of this kind of woman.

Some belles are seemingly harmless, such as Miss Iona in Smith's *Fancy Strut,* who sees herself "as the custodian of beauty and truth in Speed, the champion of the pure and good," but beneath the surface her motives are tied to power. Miss Iona writes the social column for the weekly newspaper, but she reinvents parties until they live up to her expectations of southern style and grandeur. In short, Miss Iona rewrites history, and the "truth is what you read in the paper" instead of what really happens (*FS,* 4). It may seem inconsequential that her truth concerns only garden parties, weddings, and funerals, but symbolically Miss Iona represents the power that women like her have had over the female community in the South: the power to dictate custom, to include or exclude participants in society, and even to rewrite the truth.

In the past, according to Anne Jones, women writers have criticized the Ideal Southern Woman through "imagery, plotting, characterization, and narrative point of view," but with new writers, satire has become a much stronger weapon.[8] While modern women work on gaining independence and strength, the belle stands in opposition to this goal because she is willing to sacrifice real power for the illusion of power—that is, power to lure men, power to keep a perfect home. In *Bingo,* Brown's protagonist might be protesting for many feminist southern women who see the superficiality of such power: "An oddity about this type of woman is how preoccupied she seems with her femininity. Here they were banging away at the tennis ball, hair frosted . . . and wearing fetching designer tennis togs as well as those awful socks with the pompons on the back. I had trouble taking them seriously. They spoke in voices a half-octave higher than their normal range and they were relentlessly upbeat. I felt suffocated in their presence" (316).

Fear of suffocation is just one of the responses to the belle. Some characters attempt to fight back, as does Molly Bolt in *Rubyfruit Jungle,* who locks her mother in the cellar until she promises not to make Molly learn domestic skills such as canning and sewing. And with equal passion, Jane in Godwin's *The Odd Woman* knows that she would give in to this life as a belle, which includes living "safe and secure on [her] husband's thousand acres, hostessing meetings and teas for the D.A.R. and the U.D.C.," only if she

---

8. Jones, *Tomorrow,* xii.

"had been allowed a lobotomy first" (132). Physical or intellectual death before belle-hood is a severe choice, but such satire expresses the serious attitude southern women have developed about being taken seriously.

Part of the difficulty in throwing off this vestige of the Old South stems from the strength of the stereotypes associated with southern men—which are also limiting and contradictory. In *Slow Poison*, Sheila Bosworth describes one such paradox of male behavior: "His mother ... probably taught him that rule of the Old South that prohibits males of any age from being rude to any female over the age of forty, unless she's his wife or his daughter" (212). While defining chivalrous behavior, Bosworth also reveals an important contradiction in intent and practice, suggesting that true southern chivalry may also be a myth. As Alice Walker so forcefully points out, it was not just the black slaves who were raped and beaten; the "white man's wife [was] also beaten (the slaves knew, the servants knew, the maid always knew because she doctored the bruises)." Bertram Wyatt-Brown ties such misogyny to the southern man's fear of women—"male physical dread of what seemed alien in a woman's biological functions, and male fear of a woman's ability to shame him before other men"—by complaining publicly about his failings or by presenting him without his knowing with an illegitimate child that would taint his family line.[9] Such fears lead to domination in an attempt to control women—and sometimes to the violence Walker mentions—and also to the prescription of rules for women that would force them to follow a certain code of behavior, however unrealistic.

Once these images of southern womanhood are exposed, the real southern woman in all her variations and complexities can clear space for herself. This real woman is just as beautiful as the mythical one, Daphne Athas explains, but the beauty is different: "The point is that the Beauty lives, but her vitality is in the scrapping, spunk, schemes, determination, marrying, working, and even in the slapping of other women who fail to have her guts."[10]

The southern belle is not the only stereotype women in the South must confront: woman authors in the South—as writers and intellectuals—face other stereotypes and assumptions, and again, satire is a vehicle for confronting misconceptions. Male southern writers have their own obstacles and stereotypes to face; because the South had many great writers in the first half of this century—most obviously, Faulkner—southern novelists

9. Alice Walker, *In Search of Our Mothers' Gardens: Womanist Prose* (San Diego, 1984), 307; Wyatt-Brown, *Southern Honor*, 52–54.
10. Daphne Athas, "Why There Are No Southern Writers," in *Women Writers*, ed. Prenshaw, 300.

carry an inherent burden in being compared to some of the greatest American writers. Women, however, carry the added burden of gender, in part due to the stereotype of not-so-great women writers who proliferated during the nineteenth and twentieth centuries across America, the "damned mob of scribbling women" Hawthorne found so offensive. As many of their works are reevaluated, contemporary scholars are finding much merit in them, but the stereotype still haunts women writers of today as they ask questions about their own worth. Because they are *women* writers, is their work as important or worthy of study? Because they are intellectuals, is their work readable?

In *Starcarbon,* Ellen Gilchrist creates an interesting scene that satirizes academe in general and literary scholarship in particular—as well as the stereotype of a southern woman writer. The scene centers on a party in a student's apartment at a New England university, attended by pretentious undergraduates described as "ugly dull children" who make comments such as, "I tried to be a writer. . . . But I gave it up. American Publishing is so corrupt," and "Print's been dead. . . . It was all over by the seventeenth century anyway. Except for Faulkner, Joyce, and a handful of poets." It is significant that Faulkner is mentioned as one of the few great writers to come along since the seventeenth century. Gilchrist is making it clear here, through satire, that this is the image all writers, and especially all southern writers, have to confront. The conversation concludes with a humorous poke at the stereotype of southern women writers, as one student describes another: "He's a deconstructionist. . . . He thinks his work is to unmask frauds, which is of course the biggest fraud of all. His specialty is southern women writers" (*S,* 172–73).

The reputation of white southern women writers in particular comes under attack in Dori Sanders' *Clover,* when the white widow of a black man is unjustly accused of marrying him to get information for a book. A black woman, Miss Kenyon, finally confronts the white woman, Sara Kate: "The first thing you people usually do in life is write a book. So I'm sure you've joined all the other white Southern women writers. Eager to grab at the chance to say all the things you would love to say, but afraid to say. . . . If you ever write like the others, even in fiction, that our houses are dirty, our black men are shiftless, and dare use the word nigger, you'd better be prepared to leave Round Hill, South Carolina."[11] This passage shows that black women also face stereotypes in literature, stereotypes that they feel are exploited by southern white writers. At the same time, however, the speaker refuses to see the prejudice in her own remarks.

11. Dori Sanders, *Clover* (1990; rpr. New York, 1991), 117.

In addition to preconceived notions about writers, women authors must deal with the stereotype of the intellectual. The majority of women writers in the South are university educated, and many are professors at universities and colleges throughout the country.[12] In their satiric descriptions of professors, intellectuals, and academic life, they make fun of themselves as well as of the stereotypes they may or may not fit. One generalization—that intelligence is undesirable—is tied to being both female and southern. In Boyd's *The Revolution of Little Girls,* Ellen is warned, ironically by her high school principal, that being smart will not be beneficial in her life: "You're very bright, Ellen, he said, but you've got to live in reality, that's the problem with being too smart, people who are too smart end up poorly adjusted" (148). In addition to being "poorly adjusted," intellectuals are assumed to be unhappy. In *Family Linen,* Lee Smith describes one young man as looking "intellectual," which she goes on to define: "like he was in some kind of pain."[13] Similarly, Josephine Humphreys describes the life of a teacher in extremely bleak terms: "The truth was I couldn't stand the picture of Billy McQueen as a teacher. It made my stomach sink. My teachers had always been morose because of their jobs. One reason I got straight A's in school was that I wanted to make these people happier. They were tired and hungry for love; and what's more, their cars broke down constantly. It hurt me to think of McQueen in a teacher's life. Grief-stricken was an exact description of how I felt" (*RL,* 170).

These descriptions are reminiscent of Flannery O'Connor's sharply satirical depictions of schoolteachers and intellectuals: Joy Hulga in "Good Country People," smugly sure that her Ph.D. in philosophy makes her vastly superior to everyone she meets; Asbury, whose self-proclaimed "artistic temperament" gives him license to prejudge everyone in his hometown in "The Enduring Chill"; and Rayber in *The Violent Bear It Away,* whose degrees and secular humanism create in him a disdain for anything spiritual. And like contemporary authors, O'Connor—who had earned an

12. Virtually all of the authors represented in this study have had some university training, and many have advanced degrees. Although some work full time at writing, such as Anne Tyler, Barbara Kingsolver, Tina McElroy Ansa, and Fannie Flagg, the majority either teach full time at a university or are visiting professors and lecturers: Doris Betts is at the University of North Carolina, Jill McCorkle teaches at Harvard University and Bennington College, Lee Smith is at North Carolina State University, Blanche McCrary Boyd teaches writing at Connecticut College, and Valerie Sayers directs the creative writing program at the University of Notre Dame in Indiana, to name a few. Several of the writers have Ph.D.'s, such as Rita Mae Brown, Gail Godwin, and Bobbie Ann Mason. In short, the educational credentials for southern women writers are impressive.

13. Lee Smith, *Family Linen* (1985; rpr. New York, 1992), 103.

MFA degree at the University of Iowa—was not afraid of satirizing a group that included herself.

Women's satire is sometimes nothing more than a description of the ordinary ironies and absurdities a woman encounters daily—which only seem exaggerated in the retelling. No doubt, participating in academic life and completing a degree fuel this satire, for O'Connor and today's writers have seen up close the absurdity in the academic system. In a passage from *Rubyfruit Jungle,* Brown describes a scholar and his work: "He had earned his Ph.D. in art history. His original thesis was cataloguing cows in nineteenth century French paintings and he had expanded this original interest to a thorough knowledge of cows in Western art. This very summer he had been invited to deliver the definitive paper on this subject to a group of his esteemed colleagues at Cambridge, England. Soon, he confided, he would begin his greatest project: cows in Indian art—a long smoldering passion" (190). That a person could devote his life to a "smoldering passion" about cows in paintings is absurd enough, yet Brown's comment, aimed at universities that would give degrees and hold conferences on such topics, is doubly satiric. Passages like this make nonacademics laugh in amazement and academics squirm in recognition, yet the satire comes from writers with advanced degrees and university ties, and is certainly appropriate in women's humor, which tends to laugh at self as much as at others.

After getting past the image of the southern belle and putting to rest the stereotypes of the southern woman writer and the intellectual, it may be asked, "So what is, then, the southern woman?" The question is fair, but it is not so easily answered because there are as many descriptions of the southern woman as there are southern women. An adjective that seems to surface again and again, however, is *strong,* an epithet in direct conflict with the stereotype of the southern white woman as helpless. Doris Betts explains how she uses both images when writing: "Lots of my women characters 'catch more flies with honey than vinegar,' but the vinegar is there, just as the hand inside the velvet glove is sometimes stainless steel."[14] Although southern patriarchal culture has prescribed that women be frail, writing is an act of defiance, requiring an independent voice that reflects the underlying strength in a woman. This may be why women writers are perceived as strong and why their characters also tend to be strong. Lee Smith describes one such character in *Black Mountain Breakdown* as being so determined that if "a truck ran over [her], she wouldn't bleed unless she felt like it" (155).

14. Doris Betts to the author, December, 1993.

The strength of women writers in the South is evident in both their determination and their sense of humor. Most of them cite other strong women as role models not only for their humor but also for their inspiration to write, often finding that role model within their own families. Gail Godwin's mother was also a writer, and Josephine Humphreys identifies her grandmother, Nita, as her inspiration. Bobbie Ann Mason traveled with her mother as a "groupie" for recording stars in the 1950s—although Mason credits her father for her sense of humor. Rita Mae Brown's mother kept the two of them alive during a period of extreme poverty through her resourcefulness and is now a gay rights activist. Alice Walker credits her mother's stories as the inspiration for many of her own, and Kaye Gibbons claims that her mother's strength inspired her to begin writing.[15]

Strong women outside familial ties have also encouraged and influenced many of these writers: both O'Connor and Welty, as mentioned before, but others, too, have played important inspirational roles, especially in terms of humor. Dori Sanders mentions Zora Neale Hurston as an influence on her writing, although her sense of humor she credits to growing up in a family of ten children, where humor was "necessary to survive." Josephine Humphreys describes her family as "one in which jokes were *important*—and humor was a way of communicating (maybe the only way)." Dorothy Allison sees humor in much the same way: "Humor is a survival skill, leaven to the gall and bitterness of our lives and one damn effective weapon."[16]

Such backgrounds and personal philosophies influence women authors to create strong female characters who also employ humor as an "effective weapon" in their lives, characters strong enough to effect change, as these writers attempt to move beyond stereotypes. Part of the strength of these characters comes from their independent spirit and self-confidence. Flagg, for example, describes Helen Claypoole as wandering out of the restroom in a club "so drunk that she had stuffed the back of her dress in her panties." Instead of ridiculing her, another woman observes with admiration, "Now, there's a woman who's got her freedom. Nobody gives a shit where she is and ain't nobody checkin' up on her, you can be damn sure of that" (*FGT,* 258–59).

This passage shows that the rules for southern women have changed. Women may be subject to the same trials as always, but there is an obstinate resolution that keeps them from letting background get in the way of a fu-

15. Bobbie Ann Mason to the author, January 13, 1994; Doris Betts, "Daughters," in *Female Tradition,* ed. Manning, 262–64.

16. Dori Sanders to the author, February 27, 1994; Josephine Humphreys to the author, April 11, 1994; Dorothy Allison to the author, December 7, 1993.

ture, as Kingsolver's Taylor Greer expresses: "This is not to say that I was unfamiliar with the back seat of a Chevrolet. I knew the scenery of Greenup Road, which we called Steam-It-Up Road, and I knew what a pecker looked like, and none of these sights had so far inspired me to get hogtied to a future as a tobacco farmer's wife" (*BT,* 3). Sometimes, for a woman to know what she does not want is as important as knowing what she wants, and separating herself from false images of the southern woman is the first step toward liberation, according to Elizabeth Harrison: "By freeing her protagonist from a narrow association with the southern garden, the southern woman author not only can define a new female hero— woman as active agent—but also begin to imagine a new society, one in which communal values replace hierarchical ones."[17]

Humor, an essential and integral part of this re-visioning, must be taken very "seriously" because it often signals the presence of some other emotion. Rage, for example. Clearly, the traditional and patriarchal ideas about what a woman should be do not work, according to contemporary woman writers, and this leads to humor often stemming from anger. There is individual rage, sometimes against men, as McCorkle's Jo Spencer feels when she finds out that her boyfriend has been unfaithful to her: "I told myself that one day when he was all mangled up and dying that my name would be the only murmur from his pained sorry lips" (*C,* 139). There is also rage expressed symbolically, as in Smith's *Fancy Strut:* "She didn't have to do it— there was no rush about the ironing—but she was generally mad at them all and when she was mad there was nothing she liked better than ironing. You could pretend everybody was in their clothes" (158). Later in the novel, Ruthie becomes enraged by the voice on the radio of a man she is trying to forget. She smashes her hand into the radio and jams the joint of her middle finger. At the emergency room, "they strapped it up in a little aluminum fence, which meant that she would be shooting everybody a permanent bird for two weeks" (169–70).

Anger thinly disguised by humor can be an extremely successful vehicle for change. By parodying social structures, women challenge whether those structures—such as the class system, which persists tenaciously in both southern life and southern fiction—are necessary or valid. Male and female writers, on the whole, have approached this issue with different attitudes. White male authors, especially those writing before the 1970s, commonly used literature as a way to rationalize, expiate, or confess their guilt about slavery and the Civil War, but the new southern woman writer does

17. Elizabeth Jane Harrison, *Female Pastoral: Women Writers Revisioning the American South* (Knoxville, 1991), 11–12.

not. Doris Betts explains that while some men still suffer under the weight of the past, women are managing to slough off that burden: "Inherited guilt more often frustrates those grandsons of slave owners and rebel soldiers than it seems to haunt these women writers or characters whose foremothers were field hands, farm wives, or beauty shop operators. Though Southern women writers are not blind to evil or irrationality, they are also less preoccupied by them than Robert Penn Warren or William Styron."[18]

Instead, of focusing on the defeats of the past, southern women concentrate on the potential of the present and the future. Optimism has replaced the pessimism about human potential found in Twain's later works and the dissolution of southern society so apparent in Faulkner's. And closely associated with that new optimism is a sense of humor about the past and present. *Daisy Fay and the Miracle Man* offers a satiric look at the obsession some southerners have with the outcome of the Civil War. Mrs. Dot, for example, tells her Junior Leaguers that there was no defeat: "She believes we never lost the War Between the States, that General Lee thought General Grant was the butler and just naturally handed him his sword" (*DF,* 58–59). This is not to say that southern women have eliminated guilt from their work; guilt is often redirected toward such other matters as family, sexuality, and community roles, which have a contemporary rather than historical focus.

The attitude most women writers adopt toward the class system in the modern South is pragmatic and satiric, as one of Gail Godwin's characters in *A Mother and Two Daughters* illustrates by describing aristocrats as "the barbarians who got there first."[19] In *Venus Envy,* in which "gardening, like clothing, was a way to express status" (112), Brown ruthlessly lampoons the aesthetic tastes of the upper class: "A single poppy in a round crystal bowl sitting on a perfect terrace could elicit as much rapture from Billy Cicero's mother as an orgasm. Probably more" (24).

The absurdity of proper behavior based on class or race is depicted again and again. Black women have been stereotyped as strong, nurturing, and enduring, an image perpetuated by Rhody's mother in *Rich in Love,* who responds to her daughter's announcement that she is depressed by saying, "I never knew no black women had time to get depressed. . . . You must be the first generation" (*RL,* 74). Rhody is not the first black woman to get depressed, but she may be from the first generation of black women allowed to admit they can become depressed—an important difference, and a change the older generation of both races resists. In *Baby of the Family,*

18. Betts, Introduction to *Southern Women,* ed. Inge, 4–5.
19. Gail Godwin, *A Mother and Two Daughters* (1982; rpr. New York, 1983), 241.

Lena's grandmother protests that blacks do not go to the beach. She disapprovingly labels each preparatory activity with a title "like a painting": *"Colored Folks Going to the Beach,"* "Colored folks buying beach towels," and "Colored folks buying beach shoes." This satiric scene ends with Lena's mother tactfully explaining the behavior: "When you been kept from something so long, sometimes you don't know how to act when you get to it" (*BF,* 128–32). These passages suggest that rather than focus on the past, women writers of the South want to expose the inadequacies of the past only in order to move forward in the present.

Although older black women depicted in fiction still hold their tongues in deference to whites, Bosworth reminds readers that silence is not acquiescence, when a white woman in *Slow Poison* comments, "She's a black woman in the South. It must do her heart good to watch white people fuck up" (185). There is much ironic humor in black women waiting on white women; such scenes suggest white superiority, when in fact the black woman often has the upper hand, controlling the helpless white woman who cannot care for herself or her family without assistance. In *Net of Jewels,* the black maid leaves her employer's house, saying she will be back tomorrow, "If it doesn't rain. If nothin' happens," and Gilchrist's narrator explains the significance and humor: "If nothin' happens. It was what the maids said when they left the white houses in the evenings. It was a phrase that struck terror in the white women's hearts. It meant, maybe I'll be back tomorrow to clean your house and nurse your children and iron your clothes, and maybe I won't" (47).

Such a humorous twist on the relationship between whites and blacks in the South brings insight to the whole issue of race as well as gender. In *Black and White Women of the Old South: The Peculiar Sisterhood in American Literature,* Minrose Gwin discusses the relationships between black and white women, noting that in the past, there was little, if any, bond between them: "Most of these white women in life and literature see black women as a color, as servants, as children, as adjuncts, as sexual competition, as dark sides of their own sexual selves—as black Other. They beat black women, nurture them, sentimentalize them, despise them—but they seldom see them as individuals with selves commensurate to their own." Although in many novels white women characters fail to see black women as anything but the "black Other," most southern woman authors, black and white, make it obvious, through satire, that it is foolish to base the worth of a person on race or socioeconomic level. The direction in women's fiction is toward a bonding of black and white females, especially because of the drive for gender equality, as Gwin goes on to state: "The southerner as well as the northerner, create in their fictional worlds cross-racial female bonds which generate power and strength in response to the male sphere," giving women "the voices of morality and practicality that often make white and black men seem callous or ridiculous."[20]

This practical perspective conflicts with the romantic vision of the Old South so popular with American readers. Southern women writers remind readers that just because something is old does not mean it has more value. In *Bingo,* Brown makes this clear in her description of the city hall: "The Southern city hall was an echo of Jefferson, which meant it had graceful Palladian proportions and was a bitch to heat" (56). Such humorous and honest descriptions shatter stereotypes of inherent grandeur and romance in the Old South.

Although there is much to satirize in the traditions of the Old South, to-day's South is hardly overlooked. Women writers illustrate that simply re-placing worn-out traditions with new ones will not necessarily be an im-provement. One stereotype writers challenge is the static existence of the South, forever out of step with the rest of the country. In *The Track of Real Desires,* Beverly Lowry dispels the myth that the South is hopelessly behind the times, describing Mississippi not just as up to date but also progressive: "Mississippi had a film commission. Farmers were growing funny lettuce. The yellow pages had to put in a new classification for consultancies. People made it up as they went, working in their homes at their PCs and printers and answering and recording and fax machines, dreaming up new ways to seize the time, exploit their expertise and make—they hoped—a living. A friend of a friend had taken Mell and Roy's script to the state film commis-sion. Mell had her doubts about their yuppie governor going for a splatter movie featuring the flower of southern maidenhood as the angel of death. But stranger things had happened" (*RD,* 19). Here Lowry illustrates that not only is today's South up to date but also that, unfortunately, people are ready to exploit the stereotypes of the Old South to make a profit.

The first and last chapters of Lee Smith's *Oral History* are an indictment against replacing old traditions with artificial and valueless new ones, much in the same vein as Welty's criticism of the Peacocks and Chisoms and Faulkner's harsh descriptions of the Snopeses, families that represent the vulgarity and ostentation of the New South. Smith juxtaposes images of Hoot Owl Holler—a community set in the Appalachians and steeped in history and tradition—with descriptions of characters whose lives have been altered and cheapened by modern society. Debra wears a tee-shirt with "Foxy Lady" written on it in silver glitter; her husband, Almarine, who makes a living selling for AmWay, is busy installing orange shag carpet

20.   Gwin, *Black and White Women,* 5, 10–11.

in his van; and the children are clamoring to watch *Magnum* on television (*OH*, 2–3).

After the first scene, Smith's narrative moves back in time to tell the history of the family, but the final chapter returns to the present. In a scathing commentary on the exploitation and distortion of southern traditions, Smith reveals the future of this family: *"Al will be elected president of the Junior Toastmasters Club. Then he will make a killing in AmWay and retire from it young, sinking his money into land. He will be a major investor in the ski run which will be built, eventually, on the side of Black Rock Mountain. The success of this enterprise will inspire him to embark on his grandest plan yet: Ghostland, the wildly successful theme park and recreation area . . . in Hoot Owl Holler"* (*OH*, 291–92). The misuse of tradition for profit's sake, Smith suggests, is even worse than upholding tradition merely for tradition's sake.

One final example, also by Smith, illustrates how satire may be used to depict the South of yesterday and of today. *Fancy Strut* includes a description of a town in transition between the past and the future, symbolically presented as a clashing of cultures and values: "For Speed was changing, and Manly couldn't ignore the changes either. Rows of little brick houses popped up in the lots outside town where the pecan groves had been. The Greeley mansion had been made into a library and the Bobo house had been torn down. A big neon Pepsi sign—as big as any sign in Mobile—threw its varying red light down onto the marble Confederate major in the square's center, making him blush pink all through the night. Everywhere you looked, you saw them: signs of the times" (*FS*, 6). Smith presents several interesting and significant ideas in this passage. First, the South is changing, but some of the changes are necessary and positive. A huge mansion, representative of the unjust social system of the Old South, has been turned into something communal and positive: a library. Not all changes are so progressive, though. The neon Pepsi sign, symbolizing the commercialism of the New South, causes the statue of the Confederate major to blush, perhaps in embarrassment that he fought and died to preserve a South that has been defeated not by war, but by greed.

For many authors, satire is the most effective means of making the point that traditions should be questioned and stereotypes should be destroyed, but that the replacements should be better than the old, as Lisa Merrill explains: "Comedy that recognizes the value of female experience may be an important step in developing a culture that allows women to self-critically question the stereotypes that have governed our lives."[21] Unlike traditional

---

21. Lisa Merrill, "Feminist Humor: Rebellious and Self-Affirming," in *Last Laughs*, ed. Barreca, 279.

male comedy, women's comedy does not end by reestablishing social structure and hierarchical order. Women's comedy attacks the order already in place, questioning its validity and control over society, and often suggesting new possibilities for a more positive social construct.

Contemporary southern women use humor in approaching relatively serious subjects such as love, history, religion, and identity, but this does not mean they treat these topics lightly. It may mean, however, that these writers have once and for all turned away from the shame and guilt with which pre-1970 southern writers seemed preoccupied. Instead, they convey optimism and affirmation; they look at their world and the people in it with a realistic vision tempered by humor. George Meredith stated that "to love comedy you must know the real world, and know men and women well enough not to expect too much of them, though you may still hope for good."[22] "Hoping for good" from real people is not always easy, but that hope surfaces regularly in the writing of southern women. Even though tragedy plays a major role in their novels, very often it is to illustrate the value of persisting despite pain.

Part of the importance in showing the comic as well as the tragic is that some version of truth is revealed in both. Doris Betts believes that when women finally tell the truth about their lives, "it may be that . . . part of that truth will indeed split open the world, [but] another part may heal or at least try to do so." Much of that truth, it seems, is conveyed through humor—honest humor about the difficult lives humans live. And while the answers may not always be easy or available, perhaps the key lies in making people see what they have not seen before. As Meredith proposed, "The test of true comedy is that it shall awaken thoughtful laughter," and William Bedford Clark carried Meredith's idea one step further: "In the end, laughter is indeed liberating; it enables us to get on with the work before us."[23] What that work is, of course, varies, but something all the authors mentioned in this book have in common is a new vision of the South and of the women living in it. Although they attempt to retain the good things about the past—the pride of tradition, of family, and of place—they strive to keep a sense of humor about it all, ready to admit the folly in some traditions, the absurdity found in most families, and the shame associated with the history of this place they inhabit and describe.

22. Meredith, "Essay," in *Comedy,* ed. Sypher, 24.
23. Betts, Introduction to *Southern Women,* ed. Inge, 8; Meredith, "Essay," in *Comedy,* ed. Sypher, 47; William Bedford Clark, "Twain and Faulkner: Miscegenation and the Comic Muse," in *Faulkner and Humor,* ed. Dorren Fowler and Ann J. Abadie (Jackson, 1986), 107.

What remains after the laughter is, more often than not, affirmation and optimism about the future. Meredith also commented on the benefits of comedy in building that future: "Such treasuries of sparkling laughter are wells in our desert. Sensitiveness to the comic laugh is a step in civilization."[24] By making us laugh, then, these authors are taking that first step in the creation of a better South, not solving all the problems or ending all tragedy but giving us, as Twain's Mysterious Stranger noted, the "one really effective weapon" we have in the pursuit: laughter.

24. Meredith, "Essay," in *Comedy,* ed. Sypher, 50.

BIBLIOGRAPHY

Abel, Elizabeth, Marianne Hirsch, and Elizabeth Langiand, eds. *The Voyage In: Fictions of Female Development.* Hanover, N.H., 1983.

Alexander, Maxine, ed. *Speaking for Ourselves: Women of the South.* New York, 1984.

Allison, Dorothy. *Bastard out of Carolina.* New York, 1992.

Alther, Lisa. *Bedrock.* 1990; rpr. New York, 1991.

————. *Kinflicks.* 1975; rpr. New York, 1977.

————. *Other Women.* 1984; rpr. New York, 1985.

Ansa, Tina McElroy. *Baby of the Family.* 1989; rpr. San Diego, 1991.

————. *Ugly Ways.* New York, 1993.

Barreca, Regina. *They Used to Call Me Snow White . . . But I Drifted: Women's Strategic Use of Humor.* New York, 1991.

————. *Untamed and Unabashed: Essays on Women and Humor in British Literature.* Detroit, 1994.

————, ed. *Last Laughs: Perspectives on Women and Comedy.* New York, 1988.

————, ed. *New Perspectives on Women and Comedy.* Philadelphia, 1992.

Baym, Nina. *Feminism and American Literary History: Essays.* New Brunswick, N.J., 1992.

Beatty, Richard Croom. *The Literature of the South.* Glenview, Ill., 1968.

Betts, Doris. *Heading West.* New York, 1981.

Binding, Paul. *Separate Country: A Literary Journey Through the American South.* New York, 1979.

Blount, Roy, Jr., ed. *Roy Blount's Book of Southern Humor.* New York, 1994.

Boatwright, James. Review of Eudora Welty's "Losing Battles." *New York Times Book Review,* April 12, 1970, sec. 7, p. 1.

Bosworth, Sheila. *Almost Innocent.* 1984; rpr. Baton Rouge, 1996.

————. *Slow Poison.* New York, 1992; rpr. Baton Rouge, 1998.

Boyd, Blanche McCrary. *The Revolution of Little Girls.* 1991; rpr. New York, 1992.

Brown, Rita Mae. *Bingo.* 1988; rpr. New York, 1989.

————. *Rubyfruit Jungle.* 1973; rpr. New York, 1988.

————. *Six of One.* 1978; rpr. New York, 1988.

————. *Southern Discomfort.* 1982; rpr. New York, 1988.

————. *Venus Envy.* New York, 1993.

Campbell, Joseph. *The Hero with a Thousand Faces.* Princeton, 1949.

Clark, William Bedford. "Twain and Faulkner: Miscegenation and the Comic Muse." In *Faulkner and Humor,* edited by Doreen Fowler and Ann J. Abadie. Jackson, Miss., 1986.

Cobb, James C. " 'Damn Brother, I Don't Believe I'd a-Told That!' Humor and the Cultural Identity of the American South." *Southern Cultures,* I (1995), 481–92.

Cohen, Hennig, and William B. Dillingham. *Humor of the Old Southwest.* Boston, 1964.

Cohen, Sarah Blacher, ed. *Comic Relief: Humor in Contemporary American Literature.* Urbana, Ill., 1978.

Covici, Pascal, Jr. *Mark Twain's Humor: The Image of a World.* Dallas, 1962.

Covington, Vicki. *Gathering Home.* 1988; rpr. New York, 1990.

Crews, Harry. *Feast of Snakes.* New York, 1976.

———. *The Mulching of America.* New York, 1995.

Dorson, Richard M., ed. *Davy Crockett: American Comic Legend.* New York, 1977.

Dufresne, John. *Louisiana Power & Light.* New York, 1994.

Evans, Elizabeth. *Anne Tyler.* New York, 1993.

Ferris, William. "Southern Literature and Folk Humor." *Southern Cultures,* I (1995), 431–55.

Flagg, Fannie. *Daisy Fay and the Miracle Man.* 1981; rpr. New York, 1992.

———. *Fried Green Tomatoes at the Whistle Stop Cafe.* 1987; rpr. New York, 1988.

Freud, Sigmund. *Jokes and Their Relation to the Unconscious.* 1905. Translated by James Strachey; rpr. New York, 1963.

Gibbons, Kaye. *Charms for the Easy Life.* New York, 1993.

———. *A Cure for Dreams.* 1991; rpr. New York, 1992.

———. *Ellen Foster.* 1987; rpr. New York, 1990.

———. *A Virtuous Woman.* 1989; rpr. New York, 1990.

Gilbert, Sandra M., and Susan Gubar. *The Madwoman in the Attic: The Woman Writer and the Nineteenth-Century Literary Imagination.* New Haven, 1979.

Gilchrist, Ellen. *Net of Jewels.* New York, 1992.

———. *Starcarbon.* New York, 1994.

Glasgow, Ellen. *The Romantic Comedians.* 1926; rpr. Charlottesville, Va., 1995.

Godwin, Gail. *The Finishing School.* 1984; rpr. New York, 1986.

———. *A Mother and Two Daughters.* 1982; rpr. New York, 1983.

———. *The Odd Woman.* 1974; rpr. New York, 1985.

———. *A Southern Family.* New York, 1987.

Griffin, Gail B. *Season of the Witch: Border Lines, Marginal Notes.* Pasadena, 1995.

Gwin, Minrose C. *Black and White Women of the Old South: The Peculiar Sisterhood in American Literature.* Knoxville, Tenn., 1985.

Harris, Trudier. "Adventures in a 'Foreign Country': African American Humor and the South." *Southern Cultures,* I (1995), 457–65.

Harrison, Elizabeth Jane. *Female Pastoral: Women Writers Revisioning the American South.* Knoxville, Tenn., 1991.

Heilbrun, Carolyn. *Writing a Woman's Life. New York, 1988.*

Hobson, Fred. *The Southern Writer in the Postmodern World.* Athens, Ga., 1991.

Hubbell, Jay Broadus. *The South in American Literature, 1607–1900.* Durham, 1954.

Humphreys, Josephine. *Rich in Love.* 1987; rpr. New York, 1988.

Hurston, Zora Neale. *Their Eyes Were Watching God.* 1937; rpr. New York, 1990.

Inge, Tonette Bond, ed. *Southern Women Writers: The New Generation.* Tuscaloosa, 1990.

Irigaray, Luce. *This Sex Which Is Not One.* Translated by Catherine Porter and Carolyn Burke. Ithaca, 1985.

Ivins, Molly. *Molly Ivins Can't Say That, Can She?* New York, 1991.

Johnston, Mary. "The Woman's War." *Atlantic Monthly* (April, 1910), 10.

Jones, Anne Goodwyn. "The Incredible Shrinking You-Know-What: Southern Women's Humor." *Southern Cultures,* I (1995), 467–72.

———. *Tomorrow Is Another Day: The Woman Writer in the South, 1859–1936.* Baton Rouge, 1981.

Karl, Frederick R. *American Fictions, 1940–1980.* New York, 1983.

Ketchin, Susan. *The Christ-Haunted Landscape: Faith and Doubt in Southern Fiction.* Jackson, 1994.

King, Florence. *Confessions of a Failed Southern Lady.* 1985; rpr. New York, 1990.

———. *Southern Ladies and Gentlemen.* 1975; rpr. New York, 1993.

King, Richard H. *A Southern Renaissance: The Cultural Awakening of the South, 1930–1955.* New York, 1980.

Kingsolver, Barbara. *The Bean Trees.* 1988; rpr. New York, 1989.

———. *Pigs in Heaven.* New York, 1993.

Koon, George, ed. *A Collection of Classic Southern Humor: Fiction and Occasional Fact by Some of the South's Best Storytellers.* Vol. I of II. Atlanta, 1984.

Kuhlman, Thomas. "Gallows Humor for Scaffold Settings: The Role of Humor in High Stress Service." *WHIMSY,* IV (1988), 129.

Lamb, Wendy. "An Interview with Anne Tyler." In *Critical Essays on Anne Tyler,* edited by Alice Hall Petry. New York, 1992.

Lee, Harper. *To Kill a Mockingbird.* 1960; rpr. New York, 1962.

Lowe, John. *Jump at the Sun: Zora Neale Hurston's Cosmic Comedy.* Urbana, Ill., 1994.

Lowry, Beverly. *The Track of Real Desires.* New York, 1994.

MacKethan, Lucinda H. *Daughters of Time: Creating Woman's Voice in Southern Story.* Athens, Ga., 1990.

Magee, Rosemary M., ed. *Friendship and Sympathy: Communities of Southern Women Writers.* Jackson, Miss., 1992.

Manning, Carol S., ed. *The Female Tradition in Southern Literature: Essays on Southern Women Writers.* Champaign, Ill., 1993.

Mason, Bobbie Ann. *Feather Crowns.* New York, 1993.

———. *In Country.* 1985; rpr. New York, 1989.

McCorkle, Jill. *The Cheer Leader.* 1984; rpr. Chapel Hill, 1992.

———. *Ferris Beach.* 1990; rpr. New York, 1991.

———. *Tending to Virginia.* 1987; rpr. New York, 1991.

McCullers, Carson. *"The Ballad of the Sad Café" and Other Stories.* 1951; rpr. New York, 1991.

McGhee, Paul E. "The Role of Laughter and Humor in Growing Up Female." In *Becoming Female: Perspectives on Development,* edited by Claire B. Kopp. New York, 1979.

McKee, Kathryn B. "Writing in a Different Direction: Woman Authors and the Tradition of Southwestern Humor, 1875–1910." Ph.D. dissertation, University of North Carolina at Chapel Hill, 1996.

Morrison, Toni. "What the Black Woman Asks About Woman's Lib." *New York Times Magazine,* August 22, 1971, pp. 14–15, 64–66.

Newman, Frances. *Dead Lovers Are Faithful Lovers.* 1928; rpr. Athens, Ga., 1994.

———. *The Hard-Boiled Virgin.* New York, 1930.

O'Connor, Flannery. *Mystery and Manners.* Edited by Sally Fitzgerald and Robert Fitzgerald. New York, 1961.

Owen, Howard. *Fat Lightning.* Sag Harbor, N.Y., 1994.

Parker, Dorothy. Introduction to *The Most of S. J. Perelman,* by S. J. Perelman. New York, 1958.

Pearson, Carol, and Katherine Pope. *The Female Hero in American Literature.* New York, 1981.

Petry, Alice Hall. *Understanding Anne Tyler.* Columbia, S.C., 1990.

Pratt, Alan R., ed. *Black Humor: Critical Essays.* New York, 1993.

Prenshaw, Peggy Whitman, ed. *Conversations with Eudora Welty.* Jackson, Miss., 1984.

———, ed. *Women Writers of the Contemporary South.* Jackson, Miss., 1984.

Price, Reynolds. *Clear Pictures: First Loves, First Guides.* New York, 1988.

Reed, John Shelton. "The Front Porch." *Southern Cultures,* I (1995), 417–19.

Rich, Adrienne. *What Is Found There: Notebooks on Poetry and Politics.* New York, 1993.

Rubin, Louis D., Jr. *William Elliott Shoots a Bear: Essays on the Southern Literary Imagination.* Baton Rouge, 1975.

———, ed. *The Comic Imagination in American Literature.* New Brunswick, 1973.

———, ed. *The History of Southern Literature.* Baton Rouge, 1985.

———, ed. *The Literary South.* Baton Rouge, 1979.

Sanders, Dori. *Clover.* 1990; rpr. New York, 1991.

———. *Her Own Place.* Chapel Hill, 1993.

Sayers, Valerie. *Who Do You Love.* 1991; rpr. New York, 1992.

Seidel, Kathryn Lee. *The Southern Belle in the American Novel.* Tampa, 1985.

Shields, Johanna Nicol. "White Honor, Black Humor, and the Making of a Southern Style." *Southern Cultures,* I (1995), 421–30.

Skaggs, Merrill Maguire. *The Folk of Southern Fiction.* Athens, Ga., 1972.

Smith, Lee. *Black Mountain Breakdown.* 1980; rpr. New York, 1991.

———. *Fair and Tender Ladies.* 1988; rpr. New York, 1989.

———. *Family Linen.* 1985; rpr. New York, 1992.

———. *Fancy Strut.* 1973; rpr. New York, 1991.

———. *Oral History.* 1983; rpr. New York, 1984.

———. *Something in the Wind.* New York, 1971.

Smith, Lillian. *Killers of the Dream.* 1949; rpr. New York, 1994.

Steinem, Gloria. "Do You Know This Woman? She Knows You: A Profile of Alice Walker." *MS* (June, 1982), 35–37, 89–94.

Sullivan, Walter. *Death by Melancholy: Essays on Modern Southern Fiction.* Baton Rouge, 1972.

Sypher, Wylie. *Comedy.* Garden City, N.Y., 1956.

Tate, Linda. *A Southern Weave of Women: Fiction of the Contemporary South.* Athens, Ga., 1994.

Toth, Emily. "Female Wits." *Massachusetts Review* (Winter, 1981), 783–93.

Tyler, Anne. *The Accidental Tourist.* 1985; rpr. New York, 1986.

———. *Breathing Lessons.* 1988; rpr. New York, 1989.

———. *The Clock Winder.* 1972; rpr. New York, 1983.

———. *Dinner at the Homesick Restaurant.* 1982; rpr. New York, 1983.

———. *Earthly Possessions.* 1977; rpr. New York, 1984.

———. *Saint Maybe.* New York, 1991.

———. *Searching for Caleb.* 1975; rpr. New York, 1983.

———. *A Slipping-Down Life.* 1969; rpr. New York, 1983.

———. "Still Just Writing." In *The Writer on Her Work,* edited by Janet Sternberg. New York, 1980.

———. *The Tin Can Tree.* 1965; rpr. New York, 1983.

Voelker, Joseph C. *Art and the Accidental in Anne Tyler.* Columbia, Mo., 1989.

Walker, Alice. *The Color Purple.* 1982; rpr. New York, 1983.

———. *In Search of Our Mothers' Gardens: Womanist Prose.* San Diego, 1984.

Walker, Nancy A. *"A Very Serious Thing": Women's Humor and American Culture.* Minneapolis, 1988.

Wallace, Ronald. *The Last Laugh: Form and Affirmation in the Contemporary American Comic Novel.* Columbia, Mo., 1979.

West, Michael Lee. *She Flew the Coop.* New York, 1994.

Woodward, C. Vann. *The Burden of Southern History.* Baton Rouge, 1968.

Woolf, Virginia. *A Room of One's Own.* 1929; rpr. San Diego, 1989.

Wyatt-Brown, Bertram. *Southern Honor: Ethics and Behavior in the Old South.* New York, 1982.

INDEX